INVENTING OURSELVES

$2

Project Co-ordinator: Margot Farnham

The group:
Allegra Damji
Jayne Egerton
Margot Farnham
Liz Fletcher
Nicky West

INVENTING OURSELVES

Lesbian Life Stories

HALL CARPENTER ARCHIVES
LESBIAN ORAL HISTORY GROUP

ROUTLEDGE
London and New York

To Myrtle Solomon (9 June 1921–22 April 1987), and
all the women who told their stories

First published 1989 by Routledge
11 New Fetter Lane, London EC4P 4EE
29 West 35th Street, New York, NY 10001

© 1989 Hall Carpenter Archives

Filmset by Mayhew Typesetting, Bristol, England
Printed and bound in Great Britain by
Biddles Ltd, Guildford and King's Lynn

British Library Cataloguing in Publication Data

Inventing ourselves: lesbian life stories
1. Lesbianism — Biographies — Collections
I. Hall-Carpenter Archives, Lesbian Oral
History Group
306.7'663'0922

Library of Congress Cataloging in Publication Data

Inventing ourselves.
1. Lesbians — Great Britain — Biography.
I. Hall-Carpenter Archives. II. Title: Lesbian
oral history project.
HQ75.3.I58   1989   306.7'663'0922   88-35749

ISBN 0-415-02958-9
ISBN 0-415-02959-7 (pbk.)

CONTENTS

CONTENTS

NOTE ON THE TITLE

We found the title for this book in Elsa Beckett's interview:

> I still find it difficult to believe that I was produced by my parents. I feel as if I invented myself. . . . I don't know if perhaps being lesbian makes you see the world differently. That you never see yourself as this one static being: 'Now I'm mature; now I'm grown up.' I see myself as somebody constantly able to change and able to take different viewpoints, and to learn new things.

We chose the title because this book explores how lesbians have created their lives and contributed to the changes of their times, and what the significant influences in their lives have been.

THE PHOTOGRAPHIC PORTRAITS

The media have always delighted in creating lesbian caricatures. Within popular cinema we have almost exclusively been provided with representations of lesbians as predatory, evil, tragic victims, or truly fulfilled – eventually – via a man. While so few progressive representations exist such images will prevail. Therefore the photographic portraits form a vital part of this anthology.

The traditional documentary approach to archival photography has usually claimed an 'objective view' of people, places and events. Because the photographer has not obviously constructed the content of the photograph, it is presumed to be representing the 'truth'. Oral history as a method gives validity to subjective views and first person accounts. I have tried to extend this by involving the women whose interviews appear here in the decisions concerning how and where they should be represented. I began by reading through the interview and this formed my idea of where the photograph should be taken. I then discussed this with the interviewee. In some instances my ideas conflicted with theirs: they felt a particular attachment to their home and wanted to be photographed there, or they wished to be perceived differently now than from other periods of their lives recounted in their interviews.

My portrait of Gilli came about in this way: originally I suggested to her that she could be photographed in a club as she had spent part of her early working life in the music industry. Gilli felt this was no longer representative of her life considering her current work and her idea of herself now. At Gilli's suggestion I photographed her in her home. It was my idea to photograph her on the balcony sitting on her sun chair as I felt it suggested her current need for a secure home in contrast with her earlier precarious existence in the rock business – that part of her life is suitably represented by the personal photograph of that period.

Some of the contemporary portraits have already become part of the personal archive of the interviewee; they are no longer representative of how the subject wishes to be seen. My portrait of Liz was taken in 1986. She no longer feels she wants to be represented living in uncomfortable, poor quality housing. This decision represents a number of positive changes she has made to her life style.

It is necessary that I take some control over the details of the final image. Just as the interviewer can draw out and ask the speaker to expand on experiences or periods touched upon in a life story account, as a photographer I can control the way that information about the person is relayed within the image. I initially photographed Elsa inside her home. As she moved around in her wheelchair I sensed that there was an aspect of her relationship with her house that was frustrating to her. Movement and issues related to movement are important to Elsa's life in a more positive way as well as much of her political work is concerned with the struggle for access for all people with disabilities. When I assessed the photographs afterwards, I realized there was no suggestion of the conflict represented by movement. So I re-photographed her in her garden – her cat signifies movement.

In an oral history project we are dealing with lesbians' autobiographies and we have extended this in a visual sense by including the women's personal snapshots and earlier studio portraits alongside my contemporary portraits. The childhood family snapshot is usually a record of a selected moment taken by a parent. The family album is an edited account of the family's life. From the happy family holiday snap to the studio portrait taken by an unknown photographer trying for an effect of maximum sweetness, we only have available to us idealized representations of our childhood. When the snapshot is juxtaposed with the contemporary adult portrait a special sense of history is created: the girl is unaware that she will experience her feelings, desires and needs in the social contexts of media, education system, church, state, and the expectations of parents and friends. If she chooses to fight for her sexuality to be acknowledged and accepted, she risks losing the love and friendship of family and friends. The sense of personal development and change conveyed by the close positioning of past and present representations of the subject undermines the fallacy of fixed identity.

As lesbians we have to take on the responsibility to make sure that we are part of social, political and cultural history; yet the very prejudices we are aiming to dispel sometimes force us to remain invisible. These are the portraits of the women who agreed to be photographed. Some women, especially Black women speakers, could not take the risk of being photographed.

We are at an important stage in our contemporary history. The hostile political climate, legitimized by Section 28 of the Local Government Bill, may make the production and distribution of positive lesbian imagery very difficult. Existing prejudices will be supported and made legitimate by the state. We need to continue to create our own images of ourselves. The photographic representations of lesbians within this book must be seen as just a beginning. This anthology allows us a rare opportunity to be both heard and seen.

Nicky West

PREFACE

The Hall Carpenter Archives was formed in 1982 and grew out of a NCCL/MSC Camden project on discrimination. HCA became a registered charity in 1983. The Archives contains a huge collection of press clippings, periodicals, books, the published materials of lesbian and gay groups and ephemera. The Oral History Project was set up in 1985. The GLC provided funding for a paid coordinator to work with volunteers to create a collection of tape-recorded life stories and memories. Because the sources for a lesbian and gay history have largely been the writings of experts, writers, and famous figures, we focused on the spoken accounts of a cross-range of ordinary lesbians and gay men. We wanted to emphasize the life stories of older people and people who have been marginalized within the historical accounts so far: people with disabilities, working-class people, and people from ethnic or cultural minority backgrounds.

The two separate lesbian and gay oral history groups interviewed over sixty people. With those interviews we created a large photographic and life story exhibition, two tape/slide shows and now two anthologies, this one from the lesbian group.

At the time it was not possible to anticipate the magnitude of the Government's hostility to the GLC's municipal anti-discrimination initiatives. In hindsight we recognize what a unique couple of years we had. The London Boroughs Grant Unit cut all funding to the Archives in April 1987. Now with the Local Government Amendment and the right mobilizing to restrict the freedom of speech and the civil liberties of lesbians and gay men, it seems all the more urgent to publish and find a safe home for the collection.

A small number of us are on the record, just, and we are not going away.

ACKNOWLEDGEMENTS

Thanks to: Dee Bourne; London History Workshop Sound and Video Archives; Hall Carpenter Archives Management Committee; Imperial War Museum; Mary Daly; Maria Schuman; Sheila Thompson, for the portrait of Susan Leigh; Liz Fidlon; Jewish Women in London group; Lynne Connolly, for the portrait of Diana Chapman and the small portrait of Sharley McLean; and Lizzie Thynne.

INTRODUCTION

We have recorded lesbians talking about their lives because we wanted to contribute to a lesbian history, to question the past, with ourselves as subjects, and to witness each other's lives.

To uncover what has been hidden through silence, neglect, or marginalization, we needed to ask questions which recognized the complexity of lesbians' experiences. What are the important influences on our lives as lesbians, as women? How have we effected change ourselves? We are also partly recording the ways in which women organized, met and enjoyed themselves as lesbians in the past.

We felt we could not assume we knew what a lesbian history consisted of, so women have spoken about significant developments in their lives and we are creating social histories in the widest sense. We have brought together lesbian perspectives on social history and personal reflections. Some of us discovered the significance of voicing and analysing personal experiences through feminism and women's groups.

Oral history widens the focus of history and narrows it. No longer are the written records of the powerful all that survive. Oral history allows many stories and versions to be heard and begins to question on a small scale how life was perceived and lived. It is a history which opposes the idea of the past as seamless 'heritage', one we can be nostalgic or romantic about. A lesbian oral history, especially, aims to deal with all that is ambiguous, troublesome, chaotic.

We need the past in order to be able to understand ourselves. We need it in order to believe in our future. If we have come from nowhere, where are we going to? The questions we have asked demand further questions and many more discussions. What form of lesbian scene has there been for women, and what was it like? What has the quest been like for Black women who sought a political home for Black lesbianism? We felt the need to test received ideas about role-playing and butch/femme. Where have lesbians invested their talents and time?

Critics of oral history who have a naive trust in society's written records of itself mistrust the subjectivity of oral accounts. But oral history is one of many social history methods. Because it openly acknowledges the problems of looking retrospectively at the past, oral history engages honestly with the process of history, which is one of constant re-interpretation. The speakers in this volume are very attuned to this and often are very careful to say 'At the time I felt that. Now I don't.'

Our life stories are about relationship, cause, motive, feeling and consequences – all the concerns of history. Because each speaker deals with change in her life, a narrative of cause and effect unfolds. Through stories we create our lives, invent ourselves. Telling one's life story can be a search for meaning: 'The effect it had was to make me re-evaluate my past. It changed me, actually. I think I realized a lot of oppression that I hadn't really dealt with before because I had never viewed my life as a lesbian before.'

It is important for lesbians to tell our stories to each other. The wider oral history movement which aimed to broaden history's scope by looking at 'ordinary' experience still largely uses the personal landmarks of heterosexuality to question people's lives. It is painful to realize we cannot rely on our families to pass on our stories and validate our lives, and so it is moving to realize we have each other:

> I started out the project thinking we needed an oral history of lesbians, and then it came to me how much *I* needed to hear these stories. I felt strengthened by them because they confirm a reality for me which had not been acknowledged by anybody else. I felt as if a new dimension to the past had been opened to me.

There has been much discussion in the group and with the speakers about the shifts in our perspectives. We have dated each interview because we view each interview as being fixed in time: at that time, it was so. We re-invent ourselves constantly. Some

2

women have written postscripts, but as one speaker said, 'All your
life you will want to add footnotes.' Having done the interview
some women realized that they were just beginning a process of
evaluating the past:

> Reading my interview two years later, I suppose having told my
> life story once I can now see which bits are more important than
> others and I would now definitely highlight them differently.
> You might think, 'Is this my testimony? No, it's not.'

The stories have many meanings and layers. The stories are
also, for speaker and listener, about pleasure and wildness and
humour and sadness: 'Before I did mine we spoke for about four
hours and smoked about 1,000 cigarettes.' We hope that some of
that intensity survives in the written (and edited) accounts.

Why did women agree to tell their stories in the first place?
Diana Chapman spoke because

> With Esme Langley I started *Arena Three*, which was the first
> lesbian magazine in Great Britain and from that came Kenric
> and also *Sappho*. You can trace a direct line back. I wanted to
> have that on record because otherwise things get lost in the
> mists of time.

Gilli Salvat, a youth worker, considers it important that 'we
have our own history. I've worked with young lesbians for a long
time and they always want to know what it was like before, and
there's hardly anything you can show them except Radclyffe Hall.'
For Sharley McLean, 'It's a political gesture.'

This book is unique in this country because it is an anthology
of social and lesbian history from a perspective of first-hand
experience. One story throws light on another; connections are
discovered. The interviews both complement and contradict each
other, and so each story raises new questions. We wanted to
include a fair range of diverse experiences but inevitably one book
cannot represent lesbian experience.

The interviews are now read, but they were spoken. The oral
history interview encourages first-hand accounts, impressions, feelings, and the recording of experienced events over opinion and
analysis. While the interviews are structured – and then further
structured through editing – there is not an opportunity for the
distance and reworking possible in written accounts.

The immediate audience was first a lesbian one and now it is not. Many of the experiences would only be raised and discussed among lesbians. We have certainly realized how partial and duplicitous family stories are. Many of the stories told here could not be told within the family; the family would not listen. The stories are revelatory and were told in an atmosphere of trust. They are sometimes raw and we have tried to negotiate a balance: how much should we reveal about ourselves and other women's lives in a political climate like this? Interviewers and speakers discussed the contradiction between wanting to present honest, uncensored accounts of our lives and wanting to protect each other. Before the 1970s most of the literature about lesbianism promised us desperate, lonely lives which would end in suicide or alcoholism, and we had no wish to contribute to such a portrait. By the end of the discussion we decided that the book was primarily for us, and we did not want to excise the uncomfortable sides of our lives for the sake of a PR job.

Several women in the book talk about being sexually abused by men in their families. We shouldn't need to say that male sexual abuse and violence touch all women's lives. In our discussion we were conscious of the stereotypes of lesbians as being 'damaged' by bad experiences with men. However, we feel it is an area of women's lives that it is important to be truthful about. In our interviewing we evolved a life-story approach which included family background, childhood experiences, school, and work, as well as coming out, friendships, and sexual relationships. We wanted to ask about political involvements as well as social life. The speaker first gave us an outline where she selected the formative and important experiences of her life. Then the interviewer drew up a questionnaire.

For this book we had to edit very long transcripts to 5,000 words: a heartbreaking process. The edited material has been worked on by both the speaker and the interviewer/editor. We wanted to create narratives that were interesting to read and which drew out significant events in terms of lesbian and social history.

An older woman opens the book and a young woman closes it, but we are all contemporaries. The accounts are many-layered. Sometimes within a story there is a scene or an image so haunting that it resonates beyond an individual life. One woman, coming out of the psychiatric clinic in the fifties where she has come to realize she is a lesbian, spends all her housekeeping money on a hideous and expensive coat, which she never wears. The process of finding an identity is painful. Another woman leaves India for London as a child in the same period. Her parents buy her a warm coat from Harrods: famous throughout the empire, it is the only shop they know. Then she goes to a working-class school. How do we grow up? What is waiting for us? How do we become ourselves? The accounts inform and open up the past to us; they also hold symbols of how women have really travelled.

THE STORIES

Chelsea, London, 1986. Portrait by Nicky West

MYRTLE SOLOMON

INTERVIEWED ON 6 AUGUST 1985 BY
MARGOT FARNHAM

I was born in 1921 on June 9th in London, in Kensington. I was the third of five children. My mother came from a rather wealthy but not very intellectual Jewish family who ran the first Lewis store in Manchester. My father was a solicitor, and had met my mother when they were both in their twenties. Both of them, as far as I could tell, were very different to their own parents in their liberal attitudes and the way they brought us up. We were very much British Jews.

We were brought up to belong. My mother's family were very religious Jews and my mother was already, I suppose, much more liberal than they were. Nevertheless, every Saturday we were taken to synagogue which we found a bit of a bind. You had to walk about two miles because you're not allowed to go in a vehicle. There was always a ceremony every Friday night which we all enjoyed, and we celebrated Passover and were taken away from school for various Jewish holidays, which was an embarrassment to us. So we knew we were Jewish all right, but we didn't know that that was a 'bad thing' to be until Hitler. That was the first time that we really recognized that we were different to other people. My father was 100 per cent Jewish and knew a lot about it, but he wasn't at all dogmatic about it and wanted us to know about other religions as well.

Both my parents were heavily involved in helping refugees during the war. They did their work at many levels but it was largely helping people to get out of Germany and Austria and to establish themselves in this country. Many of the refugees stayed

9

in our house. And then in the later thirties when things were
getting really difficult, they organized an exodus of, I think,
thousands of children and had to negotiate with German officials
to do that. They also started a farm school on the Scottish border,
to train the older children to be able to go to Palestine to work
on Kibbutzim.

All sorts of people stayed with us: people who had been servants
in Germany and people who'd been aristocrats. My mother had
a penchant for artists so we did rather well and had interesting
artists about the house.

Both my parents were keen Zionists then and I had no idea that
it was going to become a dirty word. As children the only reaction
we had to Zionism was that there were lavish fund raising events
always going on in the house and my mother spent her life on
different committees. My father was more interested in the Jewish
National Fund which was buying up land at the time and I think
they would have both been utterly horrified to know what's
happened since. Certainly what they believed in was not anti-
Arab. It was idealistic. The only reason why none of the children
became Zionists I think was because we resented the time it took.

We were strictly lectured by our parents to behave properly and
be nice to the refugees, as these were very unfortunate people who
had been through an awful time. So almost instinctively we didn't
and I think we were pretty unpleasant to them very often. In any
case, they weren't all nice at all and we didn't know what love or
compassion meant. We liked who we liked.

Q: *Do you remember anybody ever mentioning sexuality when you were
a child?*

There was really nothing. Looking back on it, I think that my
mother was waiting to be asked, and we never asked. At any rate,
I disassociated my parents from sex and if I wanted to ask I went
to somebody else. When I was about sixteen I was pretty innocent
and terrified out of my mind about having babies. My father was
extremely strict. They didn't really like you going out with men,
but they didn't tell you why they didn't like it. I just thought it
was because you came home late or because the bloke might ask
if he could kiss you when he brought you back in a taxi. If a
young man took me out to dinner or parties in hotels and he spent

a lot of money on me, it was embarrassing and I thought, 'My god have I got to give him everything because he's spent half a week's salary on me this evening?' I got no help from my parents on how to say no because they'd be so shocked if they knew you'd even been asked. And all I'm talking about is flirtation now. They gave you no idea how to fob off someone you didn't want. I would say I was very ignorant.

From ten years old I was at St Paul's Girls' School and I left when I was just sixteen when I failed my matriculation. My parents very much wanted me to stay and try again but I caused so many scenes that in the end they gave in. It was my ambition to go on the stage and I said I didn't need matric.

From the point of view of making friends I loved school. I hopped from passion to passion. I also had some very good friends. From the point of view of learning I can't say I got as much out of it as I should have. I was sort of mediocre and extremely bad at certain essential subjects like maths. But it was a very good school for music and encouraged interest in painting. I can't look back and say those were the happiest days of my life, but I think I rather enjoyed being unhappy; I think I thought it was more interesting. If a day went by when I hadn't cried in despair I thought there was something wrong with the day.

They had a strange habit at St Paul's: you went to the staff room and you carried the teacher's books to the class and, of course, everybody rushed to carry their favourite teachers' wretched books and you had these brief minutes bustling along the corridor with someone whom you adored. I got into what I supposed today we'd call a gang; there were four of us and we went through our school life sharing a lot of things. We had sexual experience together, yes we did. I thought it was good fun and I felt it drew us closer together. I thought it was important to our relationship and quite natural, but I guessed that we had to be careful. It was certainly not suspected by my parents. We had holidays together and we'd always share a room.

When I was growing up I heard nothing about lesbians. I only knew that the critical word for a man was pansy and as kids we thought that was rather nice. We didn't really know what we were saying, and were severely ticked off by our parents who were very tolerant and had many homosexual friends, certainly men.

The first important person I loved, without any sexual

11

fulfilment, was a woman called Alice Ehlers, a delightful person. She was a German refugee staying with my parents. Alice was extremely warm to me and we developed a very interesting friendship. When I was young I didn't like far-off adoration for a prefect or a teacher or another girl; I made it my business to get to know people I admired and to find out if there was any common ground, and if it failed I drifted away. I loved Alice . . . I would use the word 'passionately' but I suppose we have to say 'romantically' as there was no sexual fulfilment.

At the same time I met my first real love, Heather, who was also from Germany, and she was my own age. She was an only child who'd been pushed around Europe, and was much more mature than I. We fell for each other almost instantly, and that was a fulfilled relationship. The only trouble was the fear of being found out. I was a bit of a coward and it was kept a deep secret. The housemistress of Heather's boarding school, where I persuaded my parents to transfer me to for a while, was clearly aware that things could happen between her girls, and she destroyed friendships. She would make awful remarks like, 'Hello you two, do you want a pillow to share?' if you were walking together. Most unpleasant. We just thought this was a repressive adult mucking up our lives. But we were darn careful not to tell our parents. That relationship was the most important thing in my school life and maybe why I did so badly at the exams.

I think my mother understood about Heather, because when she had to go to America with her parents and I was in a terrible state, my mother tried desperately hard to get over this traditional reluctance to talk about emotions. I wouldn't let her but she did try and so she knew all right, but it was never discussed. This housemistress must have reported something and they sent me to a child psychologist and it was an absolute flop. He had a few notes in front of him so I knew he'd been told something, but I wasn't having it at all and got this chap so muddled. I never went to him again. So they did try to take a little action, but not unpleasantly I must admit.

And yet at the same time I was able to love Alice and the only way I could show it was by helping her a lot. I'd wait on her hand and foot and she taught me a great deal about music. She was a harpsichordist and she used to practise for seven or eight hours; sometimes I used to sit for hours outside her door at night, just listening.

Q: *Did you have any relationships with men when you were a young woman?*

Older than when I've been talking about, yes I did. At that time I think I was rather attractive and my older brother was at university and had a lot of men friends whose company I enjoyed. I was very flattered and I did look older than I was. Anyhow, they would take me out but if they became mildly sexually interested I was scared out of my mind. There was a lot of flirting in those days.

I didn't have sex with a man till I was about eighteen I think. And then I didn't enjoy it, but I rationalized that: I didn't go to bed with any man I was in love with, so how could I compare it to my experience with women who I'd only made love to if I was deeply attached to them? And then slowly, as the years went on I realized I wasn't going to fall in love with a man, no.

My parents took it for granted I was going to get married, and as I'd been this rather precocious young woman who loved clothes and dancing, they thought, there's going to be trouble here, and they were pretty repressive about me. For instance, they sent me to be finished off at a heavily chaperoned small school in France where you learnt culture and French, and I hated every second of it. I'd never been imprisoned before. It was a mistake and I did rebel as I was very unhappy with those restrictions. It was assumed that I was going to get married, but what they were really scared about was that I'd go berserk before getting married. I think I wanted to get married, but when I was asked the question, 'What do you want to be?', I used to say, 'I want to be the greatest lover of all time', and I didn't say wife. And then a very important thing happened to me when I was eighteen. Having been this attractive girl, I had some sort of a thyroid disturbance, put on about four stone in two months and I didn't lose it until I was at least twenty-one. Men were very influenced by that and they stopped chasing me and I became Auntie Myrtle, a role I quite enjoyed. But it did knock all the swank and confidence out of me. It was quite definitely a disgrace to be so fat and I was very miserable about it. This was just before the war started and it changed my life very much. It was a series of doctors and dieting and doctors and dieting. But no way will I allow anybody to say that that made me become a lesbian. It's true that I was no longer

Myrtle, Secretary of Peace Pledge Union, with Sybil Morrison, Bank Holiday Conference, 1962

Portrait of Myrtle Solomon

attractive to men, but that was a relief in a way.

And then I met a really lovely gay man who I had a very long friendship with and we did have sex together as well, more as an experiment for him, I think. We discussed getting married actually, but I fell too much in love with a woman so we didn't, and it was just as well. I don't think it would have worked. I was in love with him but it just wasn't satisfactory physically.

More than once Michael was a victim of police entrapment and this outraged me. I think it was the first time I was conscious that both he and I were outside the norm as far as the public and law were concerned. I became quite passionately involved in trying to get the laws altered and I realized how lucky women were that they didn't face quite the same pressures, at least not the legal ones, and I did come out in the open and speak publicly and write to newspapers. But after Michael, no more men.

Q: *How important to you was the idea of having children when you were a young woman?*

It was important, yes. And then the war made a big interruption to that thinking, and after the war I wouldn't have been brave enough to have had a child as a single parent. I doubt it very much, and it's been many years since I wanted to. I haven't wept about that for a long time, but yes I certainly did up to the age of about thirty, having come from a big family.

My brother didn't mind at all; I think I confided in him quite a lot. What happened was my family never particularly liked the women I chose and so they were able to say, I don't mind you being a lesbian in the least but couldn't you have found someone more attractive? Or couldn't you have found someone more intelligent? None of my sisters had any moral objection, but if they didn't like that person they wouldn't invite her out, so I think to that extent they showed their prejudice. So I just stopped accepting the invitations.

Very slowly I began to mind that, that I was missing out and losing touch with older friends. I had withdrawn a lot, but it wasn't with any form of shame, it was simply that if she wasn't going to be in on it then they could lump it.

I lived with a woman called Marie for fifteen years. I met her during the war in the factory, so that was quite a long marriage.

When I emerged from the war, I'd become a feminist socialist through my experiences in the factory. I was in love with what we would have called the working class; they were the only real people. I went perhaps too much that way, and though I never knew excessive poverty, I lived in a very different way and was very happy. Marie and I went away for two and a half years, travelling. We just wanted to spread our wings and we had to work as we went. Those were very happy years with her; it was lovely to have no responsibilities, no home to look after, no gas bill to pay, very self-centred.

That broke up because I fell in love with someone else and Marie took it so badly that we couldn't go on together. There was a difference between us. I can't ask her now because she's dead, but I think she was a bit ashamed of the sexual side of this relationship. She wouldn't use the word 'lesbian'. Six of those fifteen years were under wartime conditions and even after the war it was like wartime conditions. I had been having a lot of fun before the war, she'd been having utter hell. She'd been left an orphan, was bereft and poor and I'd had this lovely life. I was all ready to go back to an interesting and full life but I found I was fettered with this friend who was much more restrictive than I in every way, and I knew it wasn't working but I couldn't conceive of leaving her. I thought it would be utterly disgraceful and wrong and so we hobbled along. And then I happened to fall in love with another woman and Marie couldn't take it. It was a very painful separation.

The person who I love now I've never managed to live with, and that has been for practical reasons and we've rather liked it. It's got its drawbacks obviously and having to arrange to meet is very irksome when you're very close, but it's also rather nice. Anyhow she is a bit cynical about me and reckoned that I have a seven-year span with people, so she thought that she could prolong it a bit if we didn't live together.

In my life I've had about four or five serious relationships. I do like a full sharing. I'm not a jealous person, but I get violently jealous if I'm not allowed to share something that's gone wrong for someone I love. During this last relationship, which has been over twenty years, I've fallen in love with two much younger women, and I thought it was absolutely lovely but it nearly wrecked my more steady relationship, which I didn't want. I was wanting two things.

I have never moved around in lesbian circles. I'd no desire to go to a lesbian club. My friend Michael was much more involved in gay clubs (of course nobody knew the word 'gay' then: 'homo' was the word used) and so I knew a great deal about the set up, and I used to say to him sometimes, 'I don't know how you could bear it, all being clustered together.'

As I got older, I realized that I knew many more people who were lesbians, than when I was younger, but it wasn't talked about a great deal, and I only had one talk with my mother about it when I was much older. I was over thirty, and it was hilarious because my mother said, 'Your father and I used to discuss you quite a lot and we came to the conclusion that if you didn't want to get married we wouldn't have minded you having a liaison with a man, but when it appeared you weren't going to, I thought it was just laziness.' Mind you, my mother admired women very much, but she didn't think you were really a full woman if you hadn't had a child. She'd been waiting for me to make a 'brilliant marriage', as she would have put it, and gradually she knew, but it was not discussed, which is a great pity. One thing my mother said to me once, when she was in her seventies, was, 'Of course you've had far more experience than I have.' And I thought, 'How can you say that, mum? You married and had five children which you think is enormously important.' She said, 'I haven't lived at all; you have.' And I found that quite astonishing, so deep down maybe she didn't disapprove so much.

Q: *Do you recall whether the war was in any way a liberatory experience for lesbians?*

I think I know it was, but not through personal experience. I partly knew through my friend Michael, who was in the Air Force. Also, I worked for the Women's Voluntary Services for a year driving a canteen in London, and some of those women had even served in the First World War. Some of them were married and they were all respectable, whether they were lesbian or not. But it was so obvious from their clothes and by the way they took to the masculine role with great gusto that they were really enjoying the war.

18

Q: *Could you say something about what made you become a pacifist?*

When we emerged from the war I saw it hadn't done what I'd thought it was supposed to do and that countries and peoples weren't liberated. The Jews who I thought were going to be rescued had been by the millions killed. It was a never again thing. I think I found it the most destructive thing in my life, and that's someone who came through unwounded, alive, absolutely scot-free. I don't think I ever got over it. It was like an enormous postponement, and I've lived on that postponement ever since. At least for another twenty years, in a sense, I wasted time because it was as though you weren't living life any more; you were camping, living from day to day. And I just went on like that. Never going back to college, never learning very much. Procrastinating. Instead of thinking, 'Now it's over; now really make up for it', it had the opposite effect on me. I thought, 'It's all gone now'.

I realized after the war how we'd been brought up and how incredibly lucky we were and what opportunities we'd been given. My father was a great server; he thought you were in life to serve humanity. I don't mean in a patronizing way. I think he was quite pleased that it never entered my head to try to go back to the stage and that I was more serious. He was a remarkable man in that, no matter what any of his children took up, he became very interested in it and he helped and encouraged me.

I had developed a feminist consciousness through my experience in the factory, which I would never have had without a war. My mother had been a suffragette and my father supported that and all the children were treated with a minimum of difference at home, so I didn't know that there was any sexual discrimination. Having got the vote, I thought that was it. And then of course I really met it. The rate for the job hit us between the eyeballs in the factory. We were paid less than the sweeping man and we were doing skilled work. And then I also had to try and understand the women there who didn't mind that, who took that as perfectly normal, whereas I could, in my arrogant Solomonly way, say 'But it's absolutely disgraceful; you're a brilliant toolmaker.' Some of the women were marvellous: what was a six-years' apprenticeship for a young man they were putting into three or six months, and they just made absolute mockery of the myths that men went in for. The Nationality Law was another big interest:

an English man could marry a foreigner and give her British nationality, but a woman couldn't give British nationality to a man, and that was quite a fight. I joined this organization called Women for Westminster who were interested in those things.

The aims of that group were, regardless of party politics, to get women more interested in Parliamentary politics or local government and to stand as candidates, and to help women become much more intelligent voters. They organized a terrific campaign for equal pay and for better marriage and divorce laws. That place, I should think, was full of lesbians, but there weren't many young women there. I learned a lot but it wasn't really my milieu. I have to admit, I clearly didn't like an all-women's set up. But there I met Sybil Morrison and her friends and we all knew that they were lesbians. She was a great pacifist and I admired her very much and learnt a lot from her, and it seemed quite natural to me to become a pacifist then.

Those older suffrage campaigners swooned for us. They thought, 'We must get the young ones in.' Of course we didn't like being pushed around because we were young, but I adored those women; I thought they were marvellous. The stories they told, it was just hilarious. But had we got onto anything more private or sexual I should imagine some of them were very reactionary, although clearly they had woman partners, but you didn't ask about their sexual relationships.

Sybil, having made this fantastic discovery at the age of forty, went wild with it. Her friend was very much into the lesbian scene and knew many and went to clubs and places, but I think Sybil was a bit of a prude and not too happy about that. In terms of my pacifism, Sybil said exactly what I wanted to hear so I started learning and she had an enormous influence on that.

I first met Sybil in 1946 when I emerged from my factory and joined Women for Westminster, and I knew her on and off quite well until I went abroad on this journey with my friend for two and a half years; that was in the fifties. When I came back in the middle of the fifties, we renewed our friendship and were friends until she died, which was only the year before last. Very close friendship. We shared many joys and pains together and a lot of pacifism. She was a terrific woman and I really am indebted to her. She was my guru, I think. At the same time as I knew her so well through her living in this house, there was a lot of human frailties there. I really knew the real Sybil, which was not just the brave suffragette woman, but one with a lot of hang-ups and unhappiness. She didn't take to getting old at all well. But we had a wonderful relationship. If Sybil liked someone she was a most loyal and passionate friend. I always imagined she'd be the sort of person who'd live till ninety-nine or a hundred and still be charging up to Trafalgar Square, but it wasn't like that at all. She really went down physically.

When I came into the Peace Pledge Union in the fifties, they were shrinking and lamenting the past. They wouldn't have exactly said the good old days of the war, but the good old days of excitement and enormous closeness because their backs were to the wall. You got a sense of a very exhausted movement, although they still had splendid meetings and beautiful writers. The immediate fear of war was gone. They campaigned for total disarmament, but there was no urgency. Then along came CND and they lost thousands more members to that. The remaining PPU leaders, including Sybil, couldn't take it. Then when I became PPU General Secretary things changed because I didn't have these worries about CND. I certainly envied their size, but I regarded CND as a movement that was not going far enough. I didn't share Sybil's sense of threat.

I think I needed a personal war before I could reject it, but the young people who came into the PPU in the mix-sixties were interested in learning about non-violent resistance without needing a personal war. Vietnam made the difference. The nearest praise I can give myself is that I opened all the doors to them.

After I'd stopped working professionally for the PPU, I worked with War Resisters International. I thought, I must leave PPU before I've stayed too long. I was not at all well known in international circles and I'd only been a representative for PPU for about six years, but War Resisters were choosing a Chairperson and I stood and got an overwhelming victory. That was 1975 and I honestly think it was because I was a woman. I'd like to think that the next time and the time after I got in on my own merits.

Q: *How open are you about your sexuality in WRI?*

I'm not like the person who is going to be chair who is a gay man and very open in his peace circles. About myself, I've never really hidden it or broadcast it. But I think I do feel more relaxed now. I'm not so afraid of making a *faux pas* in company, because everybody is that little bit more knowledgeable. I think there is still a lot of prejudice but I've moved in circles where there's so little prejudice that I'm a bit spoilt. I did think in my parting speech at our triennial, I would like to have said, 'The Queen is dead; long live the Queen', but I don't know if I shall have the nerve to do it in India. I'm not standing again. Ten years is a long time.

Note

Myrtle died on 22 April 1987. The last time I saw her was at our Lesbian Oral History Group party in March 1986, when she said, 'I wish you knew when you were going to die; then you could plan things.' She was considering moving to the countryside, where she stayed when she was a child. She wrote about the interview in a letter in February 1986:

> I haven't got it over that I don't give a damn about 'being a lesbian' – it simply does not worry me. It was the upheaval of loving so deeply and becoming so passionately involved that disturbed my life, not my choice of sex. I was sorry to have upset my parents but it never entered my head to try to change. . . . I had no desire to share my love life with a cause, but it was never shame that held me back. . . . Anyhow, remember me as a happy and fulfilled woman, as I am.

SHARLEY McLEAN

INTERVIEWED ON 31 MAY 1988 BY
MARGOT FARNHAM

I was born in Oldenburg, a small market town in Northern Germany in May 1923. In those days it had 50,000 inhabitants. Pleasant little town. I had a lovely childhood. Economically we were well off, lived in a very nice, detached house with a garden, and I remember being chauffeur-driven to school. My father had a wholesale business. I had three brothers; two are dead now. The youngest was fourteen years older than I, so I was an afterthought, the only girl and terribly spoiled by my parents and brothers.

My father was left-wing and politically very active. He was a Social Democrat and he was very interested in people learning to live together. He really felt that governments were people's biggest enemies because they created a division between people, always playing off one person against the other. He said to me, 'Never take for granted what people tell you, test it. Always question things.'

My mother came from a large Jewish family in Hanover. She was kind-hearted, yet with immense strength. She was a *hausfrau*. She was a really lovely person, so warm. I loved her. She was a fantastic person [pause]. She always had time for us kids.

When I was a small child, in my immediate area, strangely enough there was only one girl. The rest were boys and we grew up playing football and *volksball*, which is a German ball-game. I did a lot of canoeing because I lived by the river. I belonged to a *Turnverein*, a gymnastics club. One could join the Hitler youth eventually but obviously I wouldn't have done that. I played with school-friends and we visited each other. We went to each others'

23

Hyde Park, London, 1986. Portrait by Nicky West

birthday parties and in those days, Saturdays or Sundays, you went out for the day into the hills.

Until I was seven, I went to a Montessori kindergarten, then I went to a *Volkschule* for the first four years and then to a *Realgymnasium*, but I left when I was thirteen because that's when my father was arrested. It was an ordinary school in a working-class area. I was always made aware that everybody should have an equal chance in life and my parents jumped on any sort of pretentiousness.

Nazi indoctrination already had started and I remember on a Monday morning we would have to go into the school playground and the German flag and the Nazi flag would be raised and people would stand there with their arms raised, singing the national anthem and then the *Horst Vessel Lied*. Without my father telling me, I sang the German national anthem without raising my hand, and I certainly didn't sing the *Horst Vessel Lied*. I was punished again and again for that but I refused to do it.

> Und wenn's Judenblut vom Messer spritz
> ja dann geht's nochmal gut.

> When Jewish blood flows from the knife,
> things will go twice as well.

> (from the Horst Vessel Lied)

I must tell you a really funny story. At one time the Germans seemed to think that semitic background could be denoted by your blood group, and somebody came round and pricked your finger and your blood was taken away and you were given a number. And I can remember to this day, we were all in this big hall and they called out certain numbers as being pure Aryan, and my number got called! There was general embarrassment but there we are.

Q: *Do you remember a moment when your parents or you realized you had to get out?*

We'd been to Karlsbad, in Czechoslovakia, in the summer of 1936. My uncle had already been arrested. I was talking to my brother about my uncle and he said, you couldn't not see that he was homosexual, he really camped it up. All that I can remember is that he was really good fun, a very easy person to like and to speak to. He lived in Berlin and occasionally came and visited. He was the youngest brother. My brother was telling me that he was a photographer, was making quite a good living at it and that he had a fantastic way of developing black and white photography. He was quite well known. His name was Kurt Bach. And, my brother said, he was very handsome. No way would he have ever hidden the fact that he was homosexual, never. Apparently, he was in a permanent relationship with somebody quite a bit younger and the younger man, in order to save his skin, laid allegations against him. But, as my brother said, you know, 'Who are we to judge him?'

My brother also seems to be pretty sure that he wore a pink triangle. There was some communication. A letter was smuggled out, from my uncle. In this letter he said he was exhausted and hungry; they didn't give him much food. They were overworked. I talked to my brother about this last letter, because I remembered it and my brother said he knew he was dying. My brother feels sure he'd been ill-treated.

My father was saying that the children should leave Germany. He met with some friends in Czechoslovakia who tried to persuade him to do something for himself because of his political life but he said, 'Oh, nobody's going to touch me.' About four or five weeks after our return to Oldenburg, my father was arrested.

In 1936 they did not really arrest you unless it was in some way political. Our house was ransacked by SA [*Sturmabteilung*, storm troops] and SS [*Schutzstaffel*, an elite Nazi police corps] and everything was pulled to pieces. My mother had a love for Meissener porcelain, and I can remember we had this glass cabinet and they just pulled it over and smashed things. My father also had an original Nolde painting, but of course it was abstract and they just slashed that.

Every night they would phone and frighten my mother out of her wits. I wasn't allowed to see my father. He was held in the prison in Oldenburg and on his way to Oranienburg Sachsenhausen concentration camp I bumped into him. I literally bumped into him. I was on my bike and they were walking him from the local prison to the station and there he was between two plainclothes people, handcuffed, and that was the last time I saw him. I got off and talked and he was terribly upset.

He said, 'Tell your mother you must get out', and, 'Look after

26

yourself. I'll always love you.' I'd never heard him say anything like that. I was really upset by that; and he'd shrunk: he was a tall man and probably overweight and he'd shrunk and his clothing was just hanging on him. He didn't know where he was going and his two companions wouldn't say. At least they didn't stop me talking to him for a while. Then they said, 'We must get the train.'

After my father was taken away, we went to stay with my grandmother in Hanover and I heard my father's name on the news and it said he had committed suicide. I was the only one in and I didn't know what to do. London came first and Strassbourg radio came later in the evening. My mother listened to that and the same thing was repeated and she heard it that way. I remember her saying, 'I must say goodbye to him.' She got in touch with the concentration camp and the body was reluctantly released. My eldest brother and an uncle went to collect it and they were told, if the coffin was opened, we'd all face a death sentence, so we don't even know whether it was the right person inside. He was cremated in Hanover. After the war my youngest brother tracked down a survivor of Oranienburg, a doctor, who then wrote to him. It appears my father was pulled out of his bunk and beaten to death. The date of my father's death is given as the twelfth of December, 1936. An obituary was in the London *Times* at the time, giving suicide as cause of death.

To him, Germany was a very beautiful country and he couldn't bear what was happening to Germany under Nazism. He would really talk to people – to Nazis! – trying to convince them of his argument. He couldn't of course. My father loved books and was very friendly with Karl Jaspers, an existentialist, who was a professor at Heidelberg University. As a child, when I knew that Karl Jaspers was coming, I would hide under the table, behind the rug which was covering it and I can remember the general conversation was that it was very important to be honest with yourself, and a certain duty one owed to the community, even if it meant personal sacrifice.

My mother felt I had to leave Germany and sent me to a Notre Dame convent in Switzerland. It was dreadful. I hated it and I ran away with the help of a gardener who put me on the right train back to Germany. My mother was horrified to see me back and contacted friends of hers in Rapallo, Italy, so I went to school

there for a year, until the Germans refused to release monies for
education and I came back to Germany in 1938, just before the
Grynszpan affair. [On 7 November, Hershl Grynszpan, a
Polish/Jewish student, tried to kill Ernst Von Rath, a Third
Secretary in the Germany Embassy in Paris. Two days later, when
Von Rath died, the German Gestapo (Secret State Police) and SS
launched a pogrom on the German Jewish communities.]

All the Jewish men in Germany were then rounded up, and the
pogroms were absolutely horrific. I was living in Hanover with
my mother and my grandmother, and my uncles were rounded
up. I'm afraid I'd inherited a little bit of my father. I wouldn't
keep quiet and they had to shove me out into the country to hide
me and I stayed with distant cousins who were farmers in
Achternhold. I stayed there until my mother had made arrange-
ment with a Kindertransport, which was the Catholic *Crusade of
Rescue* from Bloomsbury House, to get me out of Germany. And
I had to come back to Hanover to get my passport and then I
was shipped off.

My mother saw me off at the railway station in Hanover and
there she was one minute at the window, and I was looking out
and slowly she got smaller and smaller and smaller, and that
picture haunted me for years. I would dream that I would be on
a train and would try to grab hold of her. When I left Germany
it was she who I missed more than anybody in the whole wide
world. I couldn't speak about Germany.

I left in June 1939 on the *Breman*, which was a huge steamer.
We were allowed to take out of Germany one suitcase and ten
Reichsmark. There were 800 children, and when we arrived at
Dover we were met by some voluntary organizations and they
gave us a sandwich and a bar of chocolate, and it was the first
time in my life I had ever seen white bread. We arrived at the
station in London and you saw people coming up to a desk and
they would call out a name. I saw this woman coming up, very
platinum-rinsed, very made-up, and I thought, 'Oh God'. But my
name was called and I was collected by this family in Hendon and
they were all right to me. I mean, they didn't ill-treat me, but
when the war started they kept asking me about my father and my
father's associates in Germany. Of course I didn't know names.
When the war was actually declared we were in Somerset. On our
return they were arrested. I think there was some Nazi connection.

I was on my own. I had to go in front of a tribunal who asked me questions and they knew about my father and I got a certificate as a Friendly Enemy Alien. My only restrictions were that I had to report change of address and if I stayed out overnight. I had a guardian who was a Carmelite priest and I was put into a convent in Bayswater, Hijas de Maria Immaculada. That means Daughters of Mary Immaculate. They were a Spanish order.

The blitz was pretty horrific. There were all these bunks on the platform of Queensway station and if you arrived from town at six or seven o'clock in the evening you would hear people singing or quarrelling. Nights we had to go into the cellar of the convent. There was a lot of gunfire. In the morning you came up and you saw more destruction. It played on your nerves very much.

My backdoor at the convent was Kensington Gardens and I met two Jamaican medical students and became very friendly with one of them, Richard. They really tried to burst my bubble about England. They talked about Britain as a colonial power and said that if I thought Jews were being treated badly in Germany, I should come to the Colonies. I was fascinated by meeting somebody who had totally different ideas and I liked the fact that he and his friend were also playing jazz as a hobby. It was through them that I started reading about Black people. The nuns in the convent were frightened I was having an affair, and they whisked me off to the Sisters of Charity in Devon to train as a nursery nurse until I started general nursing, when I was eighteen. Convent life was a very, very difficult life to get used to. I felt the narrowness of Catholicism absolutely.

You know, I completely refute that all morality must come from something theistic because it was definitely my political background and political groups here in England that gave me strength. There was one bloke in particular called Frederich Lohr. The family I stayed with had taken me to Speakers' Corner and he was on the anarchist platform. He was of German parentage and was very upset with what was happening in Germany and we talked and he asked me, did I have any political convictions and I said, I knew very little, only what I'd heard at home. When I repeated what I'd heard my father say about governments, he said, 'Oh, you are one of us, you're an Anarchist.' I'd heard the word before in Germany but my idea of anarchism was people who go around throwing bombs. He said, 'You have a lot to learn.'

He had a presence and a very nice voice, and he started talking to me about anarchism and *War Commentary*, the anarchist paper during the war. I would read Kropotkin and Bakunin and Malatesta and I also participated in Workers' Education. I visited Freedom Press and I knew a lot of the early anarchists. Through Freddy I was introduced to Marie-Louise Berneri, who was Italian. I didn't have her courage. She had confrontations with the police; even selling *War Commentary*, they would harass her. We used to talk for hours. Speakers' Corner looked different; they used to put *War Commentary* just by a lamp-post. I went and sold *War Commentary* or *Freedom* outside Speakers' Corner and other venues and at one time Philip Sampson was inside for sedition. One may have had pacifist tendencies but I really saw the Nazi machinery as an evil and so I did not want to participate in anything that would detract from that. It was an interesting time. We ran eventually a very good speakers' indoor group at the Lamb and Flag, a poets' pub.

Until Belgium was overrun, I had news of my mother, via a cousin who sent on those letters. My mother said very little. They were very ordinary letters and you were always aware that she had to be very careful what she was saying. I learned that they'd been thrown out of where they lived, that they had to wear Star of David yellow bands, that they were not allowed to use public transport. If they wanted coal for their fire they had to walk for miles to collect it. The same with food. There were a few shops allowed to sell to them. My grandmother was already suffering from severe senility and I think she must have been an extra strain. She eventually died. About six people lived in one room. My mother tried to sound cheerful and, in her letters to my cousin, she always talked about how much she was looking forward to seeing me again. You know, to have four kids and to send them into the unknown must have been really hard for her.

After those letters ceased I had one communication which I think was dated 1942. I've still got it. I was told by the Red Cross that I could write twenty-five words and she was able to reply and all she said was, she was still well and not to worry, but after that, nothing. Through the Vatican I learned that she'd died in an extermination camp in Riga. That would have been in 1944.

Her name appeared on the list.

When I started nursing, I came across another German girl, Ruth, who also turned out to be a lesbian, and we became sisters to each other, honestly. She had lost her family, one through the Nazis; one from natural causes. She came from Berlin. We were both eighteen. She had got out of Germany much earlier with a Jewish organization. We remained great friends.

My first involvement in unions was when I was nursing at Lewisham hospital. I learned from a friend that nurses at Friern Barnet got five nights off a fortnight and we were getting only four. I heard that there was a trade union in the hospital, basically for porters and cleaners and another nurse and I got in touch. We were probably among the first nurses to join a union. You had porters who wheeled trolleys for the corpses; you had porters who looked after the rubbish. Everybody insisted on the differential and I thought that was crazy. However, we did get five nights off a fortnight.

I hated the war; we were in the frontline, all the casualties we saw. When Sandringham School was bombed, there was a tremendous anti-German feeling when those kids were brought into the hospital. It was heartbreaking: a war against children. You just worked; there was a dedication and even people with little nursing experience were called upon, to set up drips. It was all done by hand and we had a big fish kettle to sterilize things. Things were primitive compared to now and the sepsis rate was higher, and there were no wonder drugs. I was also on duty when the hospital was hit. A bomb fell on the dispensary which caused tremendous fire. As nurses we were told where there were so-called safe points and one of my friends on E Block had taken shelter at one of those points and that collapsed and she was killed outright. We were badly burned in the D Block I was in but we managed to evacuate all the patients, and people who hadn't walked for months and months suddenly found they were able to walk down these ghastly fire escapes.

At the end of the war Ruth and I went down Lewisham High Street and we sang every German folk song we could remember. It was marvellous.

> Aus grauer stadte mauern
> ziehn wir ins weite feld.

Out of the grey city confines
we are going out into the wild fields.

I'd got married in April 1944, but I was still nursing. My husband attracted me because he was a Conscientious Objector and it was a way of getting out of the hospital. The Matron was very anti-German. When I met my husband – having escaped Germany, having had a lot of trauma – he was a very glamorous person. And I was constantly reminded of being German with German bombs falling. By marriage you became British at a stroke. You were no longer a foreigner. It's a form of escape.

Q: *Did you know you were a lesbian when you got married?*

There were so many things I was pushing to the back of my mind. I should have known. Although I grew up with loads of boys, they were mates and I never had a crush on any of them. There was one girl, Ute her name was, and I had a real crush on her and I was so jealous when she had a boyfriend. Later, I'd heard the word 'lesbian', but I thought it was some sort of swear word.

When Lewisham Hospital was bombed, we all shared rooms and even beds because the rooms were so small. We were together; we cuddled each other without giving it a second thought. I think we were naive sexually. One staff nurse would say there were two ward sisters who were 'homosexual ladies'. They used to tell people they weren't married because their boyfriends were killed in the First World War. I remember we used to look at them with curiosity. Ridiculous when you think how naive one was.

I can remember one woman in particular I had a tremendous crush on. She was a cancer patient. I was very fond of her and I was told off for being too emotionally involved when she died. Also one of the orderlies used to say to me, 'Oh, you are one of us' and I thought she meant that I was as English as she was and I felt flattered that I had been accepted.

When I got married we had this room in Camden Town, and my husband was on tour a lot with the Anglo-Polish ballet. He was a dancer. Some of the nurses used to come over and I remember Ruth told me that two of our friends had set up home together and I said, 'Oh, that's nice'. She said, 'You don't understand!' And, honestly, I was that bloody ignorant, considering that Ruth was a lesbian too. The word 'lesbian' wasn't even used then. I think the term 'homosexual women' was used and for the first time I consciously thought about homosexual women.

I was twenty-three when my daughter was born and I had my son when I was twenty-six, and as soon as I became pregnant with him I ceased all sexual activities with my husband. I was so unhappy about any physical touch. I attended the Tavistock clinic because I had tried to commit suicide. I had made sure that there were enough toys for my kids to wake up to, new toys, clean clothes and enough food and I had really prepared it. I had figured out that if I pumped an overdose of insulin into myself I would die from shock. It was June and I went into Hyde Park; in those days there were a great many rhododendrons and when I was comfortable in the bushes I filled two syringes with insulin and pumped them in, and it was a sheer fluke that the police in Hyde Park had dog training on that particular week and an Alsatian dog sniffed me out in the bushes. I was in a coma by then and the next thing I knew I was lying on a table and somebody was pumping sweet tea into me. They said to me, 'We won't prosecute, but you must seek medical help.'

I think a fortnight later, I was suddenly rushed into hospital. I had an embolus in the fallopian tube and I stayed in hospital for three months and then they sent me to convalesce, so it wasn't until the following year that I actually started my sessions at Tavistock Clinic. I tell you what happened, strangely enough. I really didn't want to live, even in the hospital. I had earphones on and Vic Oliver was introducing the last night at the proms and I can't honestly remember what he said but I suddenly wanted to live and from that day onwards I recovered.

I saw a marvellous woman psychiatrist at the Tavistock Clinic. I can remember after one session she said, 'I do think I know why you were so unhappy but we want a few more sessions', and then one day she used the word 'lesbian'. That was 1950. And she said, 'you have to learn to come to terms with that, because it is natural for you.' I can remember walking out of Tavistock Clinic with several weeks of family allowance and I had wandered down Oxford Street to Selfridges and suddenly I found myself in the coats department and I was trying on this coat and it was hideous and horribly expensive. I think it took all the money I had, but

Mother, circa 1910–14, Germany

Outside school in Oldenburg, 1928

Nurse at Lewisham Hospital, 1941

At THT, 1988. Portrait by Lynne Connolly

I bought that bloody coat and I can remember arriving home with it and I thought, 'Oh my God, what on earth have I done?' I never wore that coat. It was given away at the next jumble sale. And then I thought to myself, 'She's wrong. I'm married. I've got two kids. How can I? I have to work this out in my own way.' Slowly I realized that there was some truth in it and I started looking at women much more consciously and I realized that I'd always found women far more attractive than men. It's not that one looked at women as sex objects; one was just aware.

And my friend Freddy was supportive right from the word go. Actually, Freddy found out about the Gateways for me and I went there once. He came with me and said 'Look, I'll wait for you here in the ABC for an hour and if you're not back by then I'll know that you are quite all right, but if you can't take it, come back. I'll be here.' Well I found it, and going down that basement! I'm sure that somebody looked through a spy-hole and I had to show a membership. I went in and I could see all the eyes turning and women were into suits in those days. I was still wearing a frock and a cardigan. I wasn't even wearing slacks. Very straight! And I could feel them looking at me and I suppose they thought, 'What has the cat brought in?' And I could feel myself blushing and I thought, 'I can't go in any further' and I turned tail. It was the first place where I would meet my tribe and I was horribly apprehensive and I wasn't prepared for what I saw. I said to Freddy, 'I can't go to a place like that.'

There was a group I'd heard about of homosexual women in Westbourne Grove. I'd heard about them in a roundabout way. People said, 'Oh they use dildoes' and I thought 'Well, I'll have a look. I'll go along.' They called themselves the Sisters of Kranzchen. In Germany, often woman had a Kranzchen, a sort of ring. I wrote and a letter came and they said, yes, they had tea afternoons once a week and bridge parties. They were probably a forerunner of Kenric.

There were about eight or nine women there, quite ordinary, and they seemed very friendly. Some were holding hands and seemed to be in couples. The only one singular was this girl Marianna, and she and I started to talk and I told her about the dildoes and she thought it was hilarious. She said, 'It's funny what ideas people have' and we agreed to meet again and I asked her outright, was she a lesbian, and she then said, 'Well we don't really call ourselves that but you might say I am', so she said to me, 'Have you ever had . . . that sort of relationship?' I said 'No'. And she introduced me to a woman who used to come along to the Anarchist Group and we met through the Malatesta Club which was an anarchist café, a dingy cellar in Charlotte Street.

This was Carol, and Carol was politically very aware and we met a few times and eventually we had a short relationship, I mean, that was my first lesbian encounter and I really realized, this was it. I can honestly still remember it. It was a grotty bed-sitter, she had. We were all poor. Living conditions for everybody – unless you were well-heeled – were pretty awful in those days, post-war. You were lucky if you had a reasonably decent bed-sitter. I shall never forget it. It was right at the top with a slanting roof, the room, and this very narrow bed, and in the night you could hear the mice running and I'm terrified of mice, but being with her, it didn't matter. And we talked a hell of a lot. It was quite amazing, one's imagination, and how you suddenly realize the possibilities of your body and another person's body. It was marvellous. It was a Saturday and the following day we wandered into St James's Park and it was a sunny day and we just lay there and we talked to each other. I suddenly realized I had become a whole person. She left London, but she had introduced me to Georgina.

Georgina was teaching and she had a small flatlet in the Notting Hill Gate area, and that was a nice place to escape to. When I got involved with Georgina it wasn't immediate grand love but we had a relationship of duration. It was a loving relationship. The kids took to her because she was a very lively person, very down-to-earth, and she liked kids. She knew she would never get married although she was closeted about being a lesbian; it's a word she would not use. She would say, 'It's a woman–woman relationship, why should we label it?' We had gay men friends; a 'poofter couple' is what they called themselves. Terrible isn't it? They loved the kids and my children had a really extended family; my daughter even today says she had an interesting childhood because of all the variety of things that went on.

Georgina and I saw each other every weekend. Two evenings a week she would come over here and when my husband was away she always stayed. We went to concerts and plays. We did a lot of things together. We used to go travelling, mainly in England.

We went to Wales for a couple of weeks and to Cornwall and to Scotland. I honestly believe that our relationship survived because we didn't live together twenty-four hours a day. We had breathing space. Of course we had rows, but by being separated we were able to think about it and it was easier to come together again.

I'm sure Georgina had the occasional relationship and I certainly did, and we certainly didn't talk about it. I was never aware of any guilt feeling after because I knew I loved her and those other relationships were different. There was one woman in particular. I was at Heathrow, seeing someone off. As I came down, I bumped into a Nigerian woman who had relations in Harrow and she asked me how to get there. It was early morning. I said, 'Well, you can stay with me.' I really wasn't thinking of anything. Then we started to talk. For some unknown reason we found ourselves having sex and it was totally on the spur of the moment, and you know she stayed a whole week. I don't know what her relations thought, but when she eventually phoned them she said that she got 'delayed' [laughs]. It was quite crazy and I never saw her again. The other day I came across the postcard she sent me: 'I shall never forget you. It was absolutely marvellous. Jo.'

We often talked about how we would live together and we both looked forward to that, but when the kids had grown up, she didn't really want it. She said, 'Let's wait until we retire.' And we were quite happy. That's how it remained and then she died suddenly. She died Christmas '77.

She went to her family for Christmas; they wanted her to come. She was saying she hadn't been feeling all that well; she'd been very busy with her school work. She took all these photographs and she was going to put them in an album. Then she hadn't phoned and she hadn't phoned and I kept waiting and by Boxing Day I thought, 'This is so unlike her'. And I phoned and I was told she had died, just like that, and then immediate hostility. They obviously found letters and photographs; they wouldn't even tell me where she was getting buried. I couldn't go to her funeral and they told me, 'You're wicked, you're evil, you led her astray.' They destroyed the photographs. I just walked around like a zombie.

I actually conjured her up in my mind. I know this sounds bloody crazy but I visualized her so strongly that I felt a presence and I talked to her because we hadn't said goodbye. And I talked and I said to her, 'I never told you how much I loved you' and all the things you don't say to a person when they are around. And it was as though she was there. Of course she wasn't; I felt a presence nonetheless and that lasted for quite a few weeks until I met a mutual friend of ours, a bloke called Peter. He had heard about it and we went to his flat and we started to talk about her and we ended up crying in each other's arms and after that I could let go.

It was Peter who said to me, 'Look, get into gay politics. Forget straight politics.' I was already a card-carrying member of CHE; I'd never joined a group and then I saw Marylebone and Paddington had a women's group and I went along. In Mary/Pad I was the Campaign Secretary and I would lobby with MPs. I was involved with 1979 Gay Pride. That was interesting but although it was a good effort, we went into terrible debt and I always look back and shudder a bit. I just felt I couldn't fit in. The men had taken over. Certainly I was made very aware of my age. Hyde Park Lesbian and Gay platform has been going since May 1st 1983; that seemed to be the one place where my age wasn't against me. Some of the young men were seventeen, and there was I pushing sixty. We talked about each other's experiences. How the world looks at you and the gay world looks at you too when you are over a certain age. I've been on two Lesbian Strength marches, the one led by Susan Shell [a care assistant for Barking Council, sacked for being a lesbian] and last year's.

You know, I enjoyed my life with Georgina, I wouldn't have had it any other way, but the freedom I've had since I'm single, it's rejuvenated me, honestly. Although I was politically committed before, I think being committed in the lesbian and gay scene is much more invigorating. You feel it's much more personal.

Q: *Could you say something about your political involvements before?*

After the war I was involved with CND and joined the Breakaway March on the way to Porton Down. I was with the Committee of 100. And later, I went on the large anti-Vietnam demonstrations.

Q: *Was sexuality much of an issue among the anarchists that you knew?*

What used to tickle me, the men would say, 'We all believe in free love'. That meant that they would lay as many women as possible. Wilhelm Reich was the person constantly quoted. When you think how homophobic Reich was! What I realized very early on was that women have a great deal of potential which is stifled, that women would often use their strength to uphold some very mediocre male.

Q: *How were you affected by the Women's Liberation Movement?*

We had a women's consciousness-raising group running from here. Many of the women worked for Hoovers and Nestles as packers. I can remember one woman in particular who worked at Hoovers and really contributed a large slice for the family. I can remember her downstairs becoming so indignant to think that her husband had conned her all these years about what she had considered her job and how she had meekly accepted it. You suddenly saw a woman being reborn, realizing her worth, seeing herself as a person. I joined another women's group in Ealing which was horribly middle-class. They talked about ideas in abstraction but I felt their own lives were still very structured on submission. They felt because they happened to be in professions and had made it, that there was no need for anything else. Georgina and I also went to a women's group in Notting Hill Gate. I did subscribe to *Arena* and *Sappho* eventually, so many people just wanted to read them and you passed them on. Now, I'm a Voluntary Associate, attached to Wormwood Scrubs. Whenever there is a gay prisoner, I go in and visit, but I also see ordinary prisoners.

Q: *I remember from the last time I spoke to you, you were saying you were horrified when you first realized that you were a lesbian?*

Freddy had been a really good friend and he said, 'You will understand and be quite able to live with it, later on.' I don't honestly know why I was so distraught. This is the crazy thing. I mean I knew other women who were lesbians, except we used to call ourselves homosexual women or 'good friends'. I didn't know whether I had this terrible sexual hang-up. Maybe there were sisters in the convent who were very fond of each other and the other girls may have made detrimental remarks. I remember when Ruth was about twenty-one, she had shown me a dildq and I was horrified. I do remember that, prior to talking to Freddy, and even for a short while after, I was desperately dating men, flirting, trying to disprove that I was a lesbian.

It is amazing how one searches in life for something and you don't really know what you're searching for and it may be mental and it may be physical; it may be both. With my first relationship with a woman I learned something about myself, my own body, and it was such a tremendous relief. When you think of all the experiences that you have in life! But I have a memory of this colossal relief. I couldn't come to terms with anything in my life before then because there had been something I didn't understand about myself.

I was like a small boat rocking in very high wind. Politically I had really thrown myself into anarchist thought: if it hadn't been for politics, I think I would have gone round the bend. I had two kids I loved, but that is different. One functions on so many levels. You know, it was marvellous to come to terms with yourself as a person and in a way find your missing link, though it wasn't all plain sailing. But that first experience was fantastic. That was thirty five years ago.

POSTSCRIPT

We talk a great deal about ageism and it is alive and well in lesbian groups. As a rather ancient campaigner I am constantly being made aware by young lesbians that I am jealous of their freedom . . . my generation did not really do that much . . . and sold out to men far too easily. They forget that we campaigned so that future lesbians would have it easier, and selling out to men is far from the truth.

I am aware – so are many of the older lesbians I have talked to – of rejection, and that makes me very sad. . . . And now we have Clause 28.

Sharley McLean, March 1988

Until she retired, Sharley worked all her life for the NHS. Now she works at the Terrence Higgins Trust.

A portrait by Lynne Connolly

DIANA CHAPMAN

INTERVIEWED ON 10 SEPTEMBER 1985 BY
MARGOT FARNHAM

I was born round about the same time as *The Well of Loneliness* was going to the printers, I think, which was the 3rd of May, 1928, in Bristol, and my parents were middle-aged by then. I was the first and only child.

My mother had had an unhappy childhood and had left home as soon as she could. When she met my father she was working as a telephonist in W.D. and H.O. Wills, the tobacco firm. My father's father, Alfred, conducted the band at the New Palace in Regent Street. My father's mother left them I think and Alfred farmed out my father to a bachelor whom I called Uncle Bert. My father was sent to Queen Elisabeth Hospital school in Bristol and academically did very well. And then at the age of sixteen he ran away to sea on the lower deck until the end of the Great War. He was then about thirty-two and a Chief Petty Officer. I suppose my father got married because he thought it was time that he settled down and my mother had got this obsession about having a baby as she was reaching the end of her childbearing years. And remember too that the Great War killed off millions of young men so there were 2 million charmingly called 'surplus women', so if you didn't grab a bloke then [laughs] you were likely to have had it, but she didn't love my father; she didn't even like him very much. And out of this unlikely union I arrived.

We were fairly hard up but not poverty stricken, and when I was very small we lived in a house with my aunt and grandmother in the top flat. I was a perfectly normal little girl and I've still got pictures of me at that age. I was rather a controlled looking child,

45

very neat and clean, and reading. And then when I was four we moved to another part of Bristol and we had little boys next door, who I used to do a great deal of sexual exploring with, which I knew was wrong and dirty: children pick up these vibes. But I still went on being a normal little girl until one day the little boy next door, Sydney, was standing in his garden waving his willy about and I looked at this and I thought, 'I haven't got one of those.'

I'd seen a penis before. I'd been at a mixed Infants' school. Why did this suddenly strike me? But from then on, I saw myself as a boy and of course this was all very embarrassing and I'm sure my mother hated it. But I simply rejected femaleness. I wouldn't wear skirts; I mean, if women did it, then I wouldn't. If boys did it, it was all right, and I chucked away all my dolls and acquired guns and rushed round the garden playing cowboys and Indians, and Tarzan, by myself. It also manifested itself as a sort of defeat because from that time I developed a bad stoop, which of course was psychologically induced. I stooped and my school work went to hell and I think what I was experiencing was depression, because from seven onwards I'd embarked on a battle with my body which I could never win. At seven the photographs show a butch little number, obviously not the nice normal girl of two or three years ago.

And then, when I was eleven, war broke out, which was a fairly traumatic time for everybody. I was also aware after this 'change of sex' had taken place, of a loss of a capacity for affection. I decided I was going to do what males are taught to do. You suppress your emotions. It's sissy to love people; for which I've paid the price ever since by falling in love with people left, right, and centre. The whole thing seems to have been mischannelled somewhere.

I went to Colston's Girls School in Bristol and it was quite the thing there for all the girls to be in love with each other, at least with the senior girls and the staff. It wasn't thought peculiar. When I was twelve I was walking along the edge of a swimming pool and there was a tall, dark, and handsome girl called Eleanor Ackroyd, and she smiled at me. I fell in love passionately. My passionate adoration of Eleanor Ackroyd was the beginning of my emotional life.

Q: *How was your schooling affected by the war?*

We were bombed frequently. The school was hit and the staff had
to do a certain amount of fire watching, but I was going downhill
academically so much anyway. Possibly had there not been so
many extraneous things to divert the energies of the staff, they
might have asked themselves, what is the matter with this girl who
is obviously intelligent but is just letting herself go to pot?

Q: *What was troubling you?*

Well, adolescence had arrived. I'd grown a large bosom. I was
menstruating. I didn't know who I was and I was depressed and
just a bloody mess. When I was fourteen my mother had the first
couple of operations for what was subsequently a terminal illness,
and my father also, though we didn't realize it, was on his way
to a terminal illness. By the time I was nineteen they were both
dead. Without realizing it I was living with two sick people, so by
the time I was about fifteen or sixteen, we were totally alienated
from each other. When my mother was in hospital I looked after
my father. I left school at sixteen-and-a-half because I was fed up
with it. And I went to Art College, because it was the one thing
I was good at. Then when mother became finally terminally ill, I
just stayed at home and looked after her till she died. I just felt,
when they die, I can start living my life.

By the time they died, I was madly in love with a girl of my
own age, Jean. It's a funny thing about being homosexual or
lesbian. I sort of knew I was without knowing anything about it,
because the word was never mentioned. I'd heard that there was
a book called *The Well of Loneliness*, and thought, I must read it.
I'd just begun to identify myself as a lesbian.

Q: *Do you remember anybody ever using that word?*

No. People might say, 'mannish woman'. 'Apeing a man', that's
what my mother would have said. My mother detested men. She
thought they were awful but at the same time if she'd realized her
daughter was a lesbian, she'd have said that I was a freak. I
couldn't have won, whatever I did.

Though I was desperately in love with Jean, and although we

went to bed together, I hadn't the faintest idea what I was supposed to be doing with her and I was physically unstirred by it. But I had this tremendous feeling that it was important that one should go to bed with people one was in love with. What was supposed to happen when you got there was all very vague. I wasn't turned on at all physically, though emotionally I was besotted. Jean had a devoted boyfriend and I think she liked having two people madly in love with her.

Q: *Do you remember any sex education at school or from your parents?*

The nearest to sex education I ever got from my mother was: 'Well I can't say I ever cared for that side of marriage.' At school, to do them justice, they did try not to send us into the world completely ignorant. A doctor called Edward Griffith came and lectured us about what happens and what an erection is. He never said anything about homosexuality and I used to think, 'Why doesn't he say anything about that?' Of course one picked up the so-called facts of life in the playground: 'No! They don't do that, do they? God how awful.'

What I passionately wanted was to be a man, so that I could – as I saw it – fulfil my proper function. If I were a man I would be taking Jean to a dance. If I were a man I wouldn't be playing second fiddle to any chap who wanted to take her out. I didn't see myself as female, and yet at the same time I was under this awful pressure, as all women are, to try and behave like a female, and I used to go out with men on the rare occasions they asked me. But I was never very happy with them, and I think now, actually, I was terrified of them. In those days they didn't expect to go to bed with you: they expected a good grope and a lot of slobbery kisses, so if they took me out, they pretty soon stopped because I wasn't coming across with the goods.

At one stage, I thought, I'll simply *have* to lose my virginity. By this time, I was twenty-three and living in London and madly in love with someone else. I was surrounded by older people and I thought, 'This is ridiculous; you can't go on not knowing what it's all about.' So I went to bed with a man and I thought, 'I don't know; I can't see what all the fuss is about.' Then a week later I tried another. 'At least', I thought, 'I've got rid of it.' I think a lot of women at that time felt like that about it.

Q: *Were you frightened about becoming pregnant?*

Yes. It was a terrifying thing and it kept a lot of people on the straight and narrow because, my God was it a disgrace, and abortion was literally a criminal offence. The most sensible thing would be for a man to fit himself out with a sheath and I think that's what they did with anybody they were having regular sex with. For a woman it was difficult. Contraception for unmarried women just wasn't on. You couldn't go to a doctor and say, 'Look here . . .' They'd have shown you the door.

Q: *What age did you read* The Well of Loneliness?

It was when it was re-issued as a Falcon – 1949 – I think I was twenty-one when I read it. I saw it in George's bookshop in Bristol and I walked round it and I thought, 'It's no good, I've got to have it', even though it was thirty shillings. So I bought it. I had a dentist's appointment and I was kept waiting for an hour and a half so by the time I got into his chair I'd read about a third of the book and then I went home to my digs and sat there glued for the rest of the evening. I was shattered. I thought, 'This is me; this is what it's all about.' I wept copiously; I went about in a daze. I remember these terrible feelings that Stephen has and her frustrations because she's not a man and she loves a woman. All her finest feelings, all her love, everything is just dirty and desecrated and she can't talk about it and it's secret and I thought, 'yes, this is me.' But of course it also sold me the idea that all lesbians were masculine and tall and handsome and Stephenish and, of course, I should have looked at myself and realized I wasn't any of these things. I didn't think of lesbians as being ordinary women. I thought, 'There are some women who feel themselves to be men inside, and are therefore attracted to women.' What I didn't ask myself was, 'What about the women on the other side; what are they?'

I thought I was a lesbian but then I thought that it was ridiculous and awful and every book on psychology I ever read (and I had a stack of those blue Pelicans) told me that it was immature and that I should really get my act together and reconcile myself to my femininity and find myself a good man and have children. And so I thought, I must simply get on with being a normal women. Which I tried to do without very much success. And of course in those days you didn't walk round with cropped hair and trousers, not unless you wanted to be pointed out in the street. I wore ordinary women's clothes. I never felt remotely attracted to men, but in those days, for any woman to be home by herself on a Saturday night or with another woman friend, was a stigma of the utmost failure. You were sexually unattractive and for a woman to be sexually unattractive was the kiss of death. It still is.

Q: *You studied science at college didn't you? What affected your choice?*

First of all I'd done a course of Social Studies at Bristol University and that kept me near Jean. Then she was going to France for a year and I thought, I can't stand Bristol without her, so I came to London to do shorthand and typing. There I met Sonia and fell in love and I was hanging around London doing shorthand typing jobs at which I was appallingly bad. In the end I said to Sonia, 'I don't know what I'm going to do with my life.' She asked what I wanted to do and I said, 'I once wanted to be a doctor.' I thought being a doctor was something prestigious to be; however, I couldn't get into medical school. But you could get into dental school. I did have to go and do O levels in physics, maths and chemistry. And then I did a First MB, which is the first year for dentistry and medicine at Chelsea Polytechnic and I switched to dentistry at King's College.

It was then that Poppy came into my life and for the first time in my life somebody fell madly in love with me. She was a widow; she had never been in love with a woman before. And for the first time in my life, somebody, apart from a man, attempted to make love to me but I wasn't enjoying it very much. However, I was attracted to her. And she said, 'Why don't you come back to Australia and do your dentistry at Sydney University?' Well, I have to say that, without her, I'd have never made the grade, because it was the most gruelling course. She looked after me and was encouraging and helpful. But I couldn't cope with sex in the end so I took myself off to the spare room. While I was in Australia I fell madly in love with another woman. That came to nothing. And I had an affair with a man. He was quite nice.

Again it didn't do anything for me but I felt that I was giving it a go [laughs].

I think the fifties were a bloody awful decade, especially for women, because it was the end of the war in 1945 and the same thing was happening as after the Great War. Women had come out of their homes and now were being pushed back in, and the emphasis was on femininity and the woman as homemaker and mother. When people say to me, 'Why on earth did you become a dentist?', they forget how very little choice there was for a woman in jobs. And the women's movement and feminism just died the death. I mean, there'd been a sort of feminism in the 1930s. By the 1950s it was as dead as a dodo. I read Simone de Beauvoir's *The Second Sex*, and I felt, here's a woman writing something sensible at last. I thought it was terribly intellectual but I got the message that it was saying something new about women that I'd never heard anybody say before. I can't remember what she said about lesbians but whatever it was, at least it wasn't offensive [laughs]. In fact she might have even said that it was a sensible choice or it was a choice.

Q: *Let's move onto 1963, when you read the article on lesbians in* Encounter. *Do you remember what it said?*

It was so stupid and so badly written and garbled, it made no sense at all, and a woman I know subsequently told me that that whole article was simply based on one interview with her. I wrote in reply but I was terrified because I'd put my name to a letter admitting to being a lesbian. And I thought, 'What shall I do if they publish it? I shall be exposed, people will spit on me in the street.' I was staying at that time with Jean and her husband, she'd married by then. I was convalescing; I'd had a hysterectomy which had gone wrong. I didn't talk to any of my other friends because I don't think I'd ever admitted to them that I was a lesbian. And then I went out to Australia to see Pop. I think she hoped she would persuade me to stay, but I didn't, and I told her about it, but I didn't tell anybody else.

I received a letter in Australia from a woman called Esme Langley. She made it sound as though she was halfway through preparing a magazine for lesbians and would I like to go and lick a few envelopes. Of course she was just *thinking* about it. And she

With a cat, aged 8

On beach, aged 7

On wall, aged 19

met me at the airport when I came back. I was quite appalled by her appearance – she was wearing motor-cycle gear because she came on a motor cycle – and I was very cross that she'd come to meet me anyway. I was a perfect stranger. Then I met her for a drink at The Flask pub in Highgate.

Esme and I did have a sexual relationship; once again nothing was happening to me, but we were 'lovers'. I think in retrospect it was a pretty one-sided relationship because I was working *and* doing a hell of a lot in the house, but Esme was mostly doing *Arena Three*. I was with her for eighteen months. I was still looking for love with a capital L.

Q: *Do you remember any discussions when you were setting up* Arena Three *about what kind of magazine it should be?*

We hadn't realized that there was this interest in lesbianism as pornography and that we found quite shocking. We'd have men knocking at the door or ringing up. We were very concerned that it should be a proper, decent magazine and that there should be no overt sex, nothing that could be remotely described as titillating. Just up the road from Broadhurst Gardens, our flat, lived Antony Grey and he used to appear, uttering terrible warnings that we might be prosecuted for 'uttering an obscene libel', so we had to be very careful in the climate of the time that it was fearfully respectable. I think we wouldn't send it out to any married woman who didn't have her husband's approval because I think we had one or two letters from raving husbands more or less threatening to sue us for alienation of affection.

Q: *Did you have much involvement with the Albany Trust?*

The nearest we got to an involvement was when Antony Grey was living up the road and ferrying the odd desolate lesbian who'd contacted the Albany Trust. All Antony could offer was 47a Broadhurst Gardens [laughs]. Do you realize that at that time D.J. West brought out a book called *Homosexuality*, which was a Pelican original, and women weren't mentioned. And then later on a new edition devoted one chapter to lesbianism. We were totally invisible. We didn't exist.

Tell you something else, when I was living with Esme, the

Evening Standard decided to be frightfully radical and to publish five articles about homosexuality and Ann Sharpley interviewed me and Esme, and when the day came when it was supposed to appear there was nothing. We rang Ann; we said, 'What happened?' And she said, 'I'm furious, but they feel that people simply cannot take an article about lesbians.'

I wrote an article for *Family Doctor* called 'What is a lesbian?' I said something like, 'We are perfectly ordinary people doing ordinary jobs and we're here and you don't recognize us. You think of lesbian' – I was addressing the general public – 'as weird perverted freaks, but we're simply women who prefer to live and have sex with other women. And love other women.' That would be my theme. I think that's always been my theme.

Esme wrote a lot of the early articles in *Arena Three*; I wrote a lot. We often used different names. Cynthia Reid would write and Doreen Holley wrote under a different name. Because it was around the time that the COC club in Holland was founded, we thought it would be nice if we could have something like that, that we weren't always going down into basements. I remember Doreen wrote an article called 'A decent club for decent people'. We were all concerned to present an image of normality and probity and the type of women that England would be proud of! I used to write articles about food. I suppose we might review the odd book. It wasn't a bad little magazine really. Gradually more people came in and the more literary would contribute an article. We were simply trying to put across that we were here for other lesbians to try and help combat the feeling of isolation, and that there was nothing peculiar, nasty, abnormal about us. We were simply women who preferred other women to men.

The first issue came out in about January '64. I didn't mind the journalistic part but I didn't like the social side. People would say, why can't we have meetings? And I am not a person for meetings or great numbers of people and I think Esme actually was frightfully good with people who'd arrive on the doorstep, in such dire distress that being a lesbian was often the least of their problems.

I left the family home as it was about eighteen months later; I got involved with a young woman at a New Year's party in 1965. Of course those New Year's parties were terrible because all the break ups would happen. A few weeks or months after a New

Year's party, there'd be a great change round of partners [laughs]. People used to give a hell of a lot of parties in those days and everybody did a hell of a lot of drinking. I used to say to Doreen, What was that party like? And she'd say, 'Well, Diana, it was one of those parties where there would be somebody being sick in the bathroom and a couple snogging in the bedroom and somebody crying in the hall' [laughs]. I used to invariably end up standing in the kitchen chatting with Doreen.

We used to go to the Gateways too, and there was at that stage a club which we liked slightly better called the Robin Hood, in Inverness Terrace, but that closed. They were basements and, in those days, you didn't have these bloody awful juke boxes so that if you went there to meet people you could talk to them.

Q: *Moving on to the formation of Kenric and the meetings at the Shakespeare's Head. Do you remember what things were discussed at those meetings?*

I remember we had a very bitter debate on whether women should come dressed as men. A lot of women would dash home, chuck off their step-ins and Brylcreem their hair and get into gents' natty suitings, but their friends would dress in an exaggeratedly female way. But then there were always people like me and Esme who just dressed in slacks and a shirt. I said I certainly didn't think everybody's got to come looking like a 'normal' woman, but I preferred people not to look too extremely masculine because we had to go through the public bar. We couldn't say we were a group of lesbians, we used to make out we were a group of businesswomen out on the town.

Kenric was formed in 1965. I walked out on Esme that year and that precipitated a crisis. People who formed the basis of the Kensington and Richmond group then said, Esme's being difficult about all this and we'll form a new group and call it Kenric. I think people wanted to help and take over a bit and Esme just wanted to keep it all herself and she made *Arena Three* into a limited company. There was a meeting in a room at the House of Commons in which all the interested parties were going to thrash out this business of *Arena Three*/Kenric. And Esme didn't come, so everybody was disgusted and went off and formed Kenric. I joined and went to one or two of their functions, but I was never part of setting it up.

I remember in, I think, 1971, a group of doctors from the Maudsley raised about fifty volunteers from Kenric because they were concerned to discover whether there were any measurable anatomical physiological differences between lesbians and straight women. And we all assembled at some medical centre in Bloomsbury and were asked to strip off. I think maybe we were allowed to keep our knickers on. It was all extremely embarrassing and somebody remarked that it was the most uninhibited Kenric party they'd ever been to. We had to bring along a 24-hour specimen of urine and they photographed us, measured the subcutaneous fat and took buccal smears from the inside of our cheek. We also answered a psychological questionnaire. And then we dressed and went home and heard nothing more until eighteen months later they were pressed to come and talk to us. It transpired that they could find no significant differences except that lesbians were inclined to start menstruating a little bit later. What they did say, though, was that lesbians evinced far worse relationships with their parents than the straight women did; we hate our parents. Now they would probably redesign the test. All these tests were probably based on certain assumptions about men and women that would no longer be considered valid.

From Kenric itself, people wanted a social thing; nobody would have touched a magazine after what happened with *Arena Three*, until Jackie started *Sappho*. I'd heard of this magazine *Sappho* and I remember someone ringing me up and saying they were giving a benefit disco and why didn't I come. Rosie and I together started writing for it. That must have been 1973. I wrote the monthly Amazon column. I used to write about anything that came into my head. Mostly something light, sometimes serious if I felt impassioned about something. I did enjoy it, though I used to feel it a strain that I had to turn it out every month and Jackie would ring up and say, 'Oh darling, we are waiting for another Amazon!'

I think isolated people living in parts of Great Britain where they had no contact with other lesbians read it. You'd get sad letters saying, 'My girlfriend and I live in Clwyd and nobody knows we're gay and it's such a lifeline to get *Sappho*.' I think it was probably a middle-class readership, by and large. Jackie used to say that nobody ever bought it to read, they only bought it for the contact ads [laughs]. There'd be about a dozen every month

and they all invariably said: 'Kind-hearted woman who loves
animals and likes the country, good meals, cooking and the
civilized life, would like to meet similar for warm friendship.' And
I used to think, I don't know why these warm, lovely people don't
get together. Those of us in London helped out with the post and
a lot of people would give their time in the office. I suppose half
a dozen women were there laying the magazine out, getting it
printed and distributed, with Jackie masterminding it.

The monthly meetings started off in the Euston Tavern in about
'73. They were quite pleasant those meetings; we had discussions
and then everybody would break up and have a drink and talk.

Q: *How were you affected by the political changes of the late sixties,
early seventies, like the Women's Liberation Movement?*

I thought it was absolutely marvellous. My nearest contact with
feminism had been *Sappho* which always described itself as a
lesbian feminist magazine and had a feminist slant, something that
at that time Kenric did not. What I wasn't so keen on was the
Gay Liberation Front. You see, I am a deeply conservative
person, with a small c, and I didn't like that kind of brashness and
anger. As I say, I'd spent my life saying, 'No, no, no; we're just
like everybody else' and here were all these terrible people making
out that we were not. It was a completely different generation. I'd
defend their right to do it and good luck to them, but it wasn't
anything that I would have been part of. In fact I remember once
[laughs] when the GLF was being particularly offensive and a
friend, Hilary said, 'But I don't feel that I do want to identify
with the Gay Liberation Front. I feel more like identifying with
The Townswomen's Guild!' [laughs]. And I think that's how the
older generation of us feel and there's an older generation still, like
a friend of mine in her seventies who doesn't believe in any flag-
waving at all. She thinks it's all got to be terribly discreet, dear,
but you have your little affairs and all the girls know who each
other are. And I'd say, 'But Zenka, people are terribly isolated.'
But she never was.

Q: *Earlier you were talking about invisibility. How were you affected by that in your own life?*

Oh very much, because whatever job you were doing, one's social milieu tended to be amongst lesbians. Friends of long standing who were heterosexual knew that I was a lesbian, but when it came to work it always seemed to me that you give the appearance of being a very lonely person having no social life at all, because you can't talk about it. And of course another awful aspect of it is if you're desperately upset. If you're a straight woman you can say, 'Oh my God, he's gone off with another woman, I feel so terrible.' And they'd all say, 'Oh, he's treating her so badly, the swine.' But you could be bleeding from the ears but had to keep quiet about everything.

The first thing I found when I met other lesbians was that none of us had ever been able to talk to anybody else. There'd be a great outpouring of what it was like and what we'd been through.

POSTSCRIPT

If this brief life comes across, at least in its early days, as bleak, it is no more so than that of thousands of gay women and men of my generation. Now, Thatcher's government, by way of the infamous Section 28, is trying to push us all back to those pre-1960s days of 'lies, secrets, silence'.

At our age, we no longer have to cower in the shadows, fearful of our jobs; we have nothing to lose but our gains. My message to the grey homophobes at Westminster is simply this: WE ARE NOT GOING BACK INTO THE CLOSET.

Diana Chapman, 3 March 1988

ELSA BECKETT

INTERVIEWED IN OCTOBER 1985 BY J.

I was born in Zambia which was then Northern Rhodesia, in 1939. My mother was a Londoner and my father was South African. He got a job up on the copper belt and my brothers and I were born up there. My father was a very sad person, very unable to express emotion and, really, I don't know what drew him and my mother together. I used to say to her sometimes, 'Why did you marry him?' And she'd say, 'Well, I wanted to have you children.' She was thirty-seven when I was born and I was the oldest. Even now, I see my mother as being younger than I am. I have this feeling about her that she's a very, kind of, innocent person. I think she did realize that she and my father were incompatible before they married but I think women were rather pressured into achieving through marriage, although she'd always been self-supporting. I remember once she said to me, 'Oh, if only, once we'd had the children, the men would just go off, would just leave, how pleasant it would be.'

I was also brought up with Black men. They didn't spend time with us but they were there in the garden, working and chopping wood. They saw that we didn't run into the road. I remember feeling very indignant once when a young boy who looked after us had to go back to his mother because she was missing him. I thought, 'He's here to be with us.' Families were separated. The women stayed in the village and the men came into the mining camps or worked as house servants. I was treated with great respect by these men. One of them once said, 'Oh, Miss Elsa's very clever' and that was the best praise I'd ever had. I didn't get it from my parents at all.

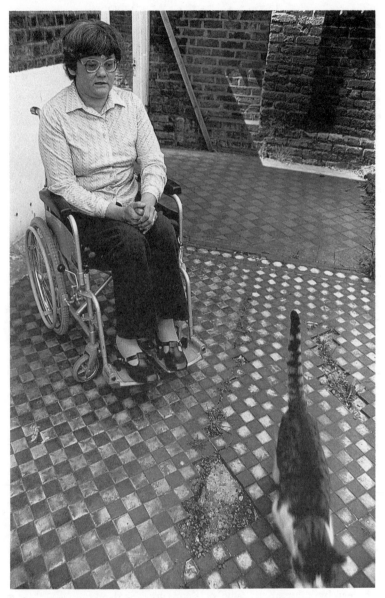

Forest Gate, London, 1986. Portrait by Nicky West

ELSA BECKETT

When I was about five or six, I began a very intense friendship with one girl because we had a lot in common. We had a great saga, a soap opera going on with our dolls and there were these two families of dolls who travelled around together. I suppose it was sort of voortrekker stuff, but with no men. Oh yes, the men were absolute idiots and the boy dolls were extremely foolish. I remember the women were very strong; they did all the travel arrangements and were in charge of the families. I used to look forward to these meetings with her, about once a week perhaps. And suddenly it all came to an end. She wasn't invited to my house any more and I wasn't invited to hers and I was very puzzled by this. I did arrange one meeting with her once, but it was just futile. I realized then that the friendship hadn't meant as much to her as it did to me. When I was in my late teens I realized why this friendship had been ended by our mothers and I got very angry about it. They had stopped a simple relationship because of what they had read into it.

Later at school, I just had one other friend, Jean, and the two of us were together most of the time.

When I was fourteen or fifteen our class did a play and none of the boys would take part. Our male English teacher organized us. The play was *Queer Street*, about a burglar's daughter who becomes engaged to a policeman and the embarrassment and deception when he comes to tea. Of course, it transpires in the end that this policeman is really a burglar, trying to impress them and in the end he is arrested by a real policeman. I chose the part of the burglar–policeman and, although I wasn't attracted to the girl who played the fiancee, I found the part very enjoyable, looking at her soulfully, draping my arm over the back of her chair and talking to her in a voice supposed to indicate barely suppressed desire. It was fun being the person making the advances and I really threw myself into the part. If I had done more acting like this I think I would have done something about being lesbian a lot earlier.

And then I met Kathryn at one of Jean's tea parties. I must have been fourteen and Kathryn was nineteen then. She was already working in the mine offices. Jean and I had great respect for Kathryn. She was very unusual. She wasn't like the other girls or young women on the mine, because she didn't wear make-up. She wasn't very fussy about clothes and she didn't have

61

boyfriends. Kathryn was very much against attracting men.

In my last year at school, my parents moved south again and my teachers persuaded my father that it wouldn't be a very good idea for me to leave school in my last year. So I stayed with Jean and saw a lot of Kathryn in my last year at school, when I was sixteen. And every weekend we used to go to Kathryn's. Her parents would be out and she used to cook a meal for us. This was really the highlight of the week for me. It was a sort of heroine worship, I suppose. And I thought, 'What I would really like is to spend the rest of my life with Kathryn.' I remember thinking that but discounting it almost immediately because I thought, 'Women just don't do this.' I also thought, 'Kathryn wouldn't possibly want to live with me.' She seemed so much above me because she's very clever. Very widely read, very intellectual and very unphysical. I mean she wasn't the sort of person who would touch you or kiss you. And that was one of the difficulties in our relationship, that there wasn't this kind of free and easy physical contact that women have, just in friendship. So it was a big step to try and overcome that.

I remember once she was sitting on a settee and I was sitting on the carpet at her feet and my head was very near her knee. And I just wanted to lean sideways and put my head on her knee. I remember that feeling so strongly and I just couldn't do it. Because I suppose I feared being pushed away. Actually, she wouldn't have, because she wanted that too, but neither of us could bridge this gap.

And of course there were no books in our library that had anything about lesbians in them. Perhaps if I had the chance to read something about other women then I would have thought, 'Oh yes, other women do this.' But it just didn't connect with me at all.

So as that year came to an end and I was going to go down to college, I said to Kathryn, 'Shall we write to each other?' And she said, 'Oh yes, I'd like to do that.' And I remember I could hardly get on the train fast enough to start writing these letters. Mostly, you see, we weren't alone together, so these letters seemed so important because they were private, they were just between us. I didn't realize how long it was going to go on, but for about ten years until we met again, we were writing to each other mostly every week. We wrote about everything except the important thing between us. Politics and books and everyday life. In a way I think what a dreadful waste of time all those years were, but I also think I was such an immature person when I was sixteen or seventeen. I don't think it would have been fair on Kathryn to take me on then.

Then I was at college – and then I broke my back in 1957 and became a paraplegic. After that I came to England and went to Stoke Mandeville to be rehabilitated. It was a great disappointment, really, being at Stoke, because I thought I was going to be trained in a job and that I would become independent. I tried to teach myself to type on a horrendous little machine. There was a great bench full of rusty old clocks. So, as far as getting me back into the world it was a pretty useless experience. I learned the basic things like bladder and bowel control but really I think that could have been taught at any hospital.

I didn't want to go home because I thought, 'Now I'm disabled, I'll be stuck at home all the time, with absolutely no way of escaping.' I hadn't been trained for a job so I asked the doctors if I could stay there in London, move into a hostel, get some training and get a job. They said, 'No, you're only eighteen; you've got to go back to your parents and start life from there.'

I argued with them as best I could but they did not take me seriously, so I thought the only thing to do was to get married. I wouldn't say that I was anti-men at all, but none of my friendships had ever been with men. Looking back, it really was like a nightmare: that I could suddenly start being very pleasant to a man and get enmeshed and engaged and married. I now see that, having become disabled, I was trying to be a real woman. I remember suddenly becoming a sort of teenager and being interested in all kinds of teenage things. I think my personality changed for quite a few years after I became disabled, because I was trying to prove that I was female I think. In our society you do that by getting married and having children, don't you?

Well, my parents didn't like him and the marriage itself lasted three months. It dragged on for two years but as a marriage it lasted three months. Really I was lucky in that I married somebody incompatible and totally unsuitable because otherwise I could be like quite a few of the women that I'm in correspondence with now, who married a man who was very nice and gentle and they now know they're lesbian but they can't leave him. They feel they're betraying him if they desert him now because he's given them a lot. So perhaps there was method in my madness in choosing somebody who was really unsuitable.

That marriage came to an end and I still had no training for anything. So I wrote to my father and asked if I could come home. I went back but things were going very badly between him and my mother and all the usual rows started. I did my best to fit in because I had no money of my own and no chance of getting any but I felt like an anaesthetized person. I still really wasn't myself. I wrote a great deal but very little of it got published.

And then, about 1964, my father bought a smallholding in Southern Rhodesia and so we went down there to live. My father had become sort of fascist at this time. It was rather strange. All my childhood he'd been a democrat and totally out of step with everybody else in Rhodesia. I suppose he became more and more bitter because the political climate changed. My mother was a kind of watercolour person in that relationship and my father was the one you had to placate all the time.

I did see Kathryn a few times and it's strange that we both had phones but we never dreamed of telephoning each other. She hates the phone, but with me I think it was because I couldn't pay for my own phone bills. The awful thing about women who haven't got their own money is it restricts so much what you actually do, doesn't it? I mean, during my marriage, I couldn't write to her as much as I had before simply because I wasn't paying for the postage. There was so little money. I mean, there was money for my husband for the things he wanted to do but not for myself.

At about this time, Kathryn spent a week at my parents' smallholding. My youngest brother had got engaged to a woman five years older than himself and my father was enraged about this. He said, 'We've got to go down and stop this marriage going ahead', and I dreaded it because I thought about all the problems of access and the toilets on the way to South Africa. Kathryn was working in the police but was leaving the service at that time to come to Britain permanently, and she had this leave time. So I said, 'Can I stay on the farm if Kathryn stays with me for the week?' So off they went and Kathryn came down, and I had been thinking for some time that I was really coming to terms with myself at last. I was getting the *New Statesman* and I remember this article by Brian McGee called 'One in Twenty' which I read with great interest. When I finished it I suddenly realized that this article had been about me, that I was this person called a lesbian and I remember feeling quite cold and frightened reading this word. It was the first time I connected the word with me, that this was a word that other people would use about me.

So I thought, 'Well, I can now say something to Kathryn. She's no longer going to be on the continent of Africa so if she doesn't like what I tell her, she can say, "We're not going to write about that".' She'd have this distance. But all through the week I couldn't say anything. I suppose I was frightened of scenes and rows because there were so many of them with my father. I waited until the weekend when my parents got back from South Africa. Kathryn and I were still sharing a room, and I said, 'You know we can't talk like this because my mother can hear. Will you come in bed and sit with me?' So Kathryn did and I put my arm around her and covered her up. And she said afterwards that if nothing else had happened, she would have remembered that forever. And then I kissed her. After that it was all right. And we talked and talked and we decided we would live together if we could. We were exhausted in the morning. We had just two or three days together and then she flew to England.

I didn't come to England until 1969, so for three years we were still writing to each other. My mother once said, 'I think I ought to know what's going on in these letters.' I said, 'Oh, nothing you would understand.' After my accident she had dealt with all my books and papers and had to tear up things and she said, 'I have read your letters from Kathryn and I think this friendship is very unhealthy.' And I just laughed. It was just a hilarious use of this word.

During those three years I went to stay with some friends who had a lot of daughters, and some were teenagers and this was another time when people wanted to talk about lesbians and I thought, 'God, they know. They're trying to get me to say something.' I didn't because this was rather a gossipy family. The mother of the family said to me, 'I've got these friends and he's queer and she's queer. They're a couple. They've got two children but they're both queer.' And I pretended I didn't know what she meant. There was absolutely nothing on radio or television about gay people at all. Years later, I learned that there'd been a drama group on the copper belt and apparently they all knew what

Aged 4/5 Northern Rhodesia

Aged 5 with brother Alan in Northern Rhodesia

Aged 16/17 with brothers and their friend in South Africa

homosexuality was. And I was very annoyed because I thought, 'Well, they kept it to themselves.'

Kathryn used to go on leave to Britain every couple of years when she was in the police, and she joined the Minorities Research Group, went to their meetings and supported them financially as well. Looking back I think there were various people who were homosexual. There were a lot of suicides for such a small community, which people would blame on the weather. They would say that the build-up to the rains, this tremendous heat in October, made people shoot themselves and it was dismissed as that. But there was one man who shot himself who my mother made a point of telling me about. She said, 'Well, why he shot himself was that he wasn't really a man. He wasn't quite a man.' And I thought, 'Oh, he must have had a bit of penis missing.'

It really was a very stifling sort of society, I realize now. And I think any homosexuals who found themselves there either got out or joined the drama group if they knew about it. I suppose it's no use feeling angry about the amount of ignorance, but I really feel that my life was held back so much. Just out of sheer ignorance. Perhaps if I'd been a more sexual person I would have gone looking for information, but I don't think I was. Affection and love are very much more important to me. From when I was about eight years old I can remember praying, 'I hope somebody will love me.'

The strange thing is that there were positive things about homosexuality when I was a child, because my father had lots of books and he never stopped us reading anything. I remember one book which had tasteful descriptions of men but there were no descriptions of women at all. And yet, in our culture, there must be a hint somewhere or other, because when Kathryn and I first knowingly met two other lesbians, we were both very frightened. I thought, 'They'll be predatory; they'll be aggressive, they'll try to split us up.' And of course the minute I met them, no such thing. They were exactly like us. I cannot see where it came from, this horrible picture which we knew was not true of us, but which we thought was of others.

Going along like this, it strikes me that I never ever felt guilty about being a lesbian. I think I taught myself to feel guilty about sexual feeling for about a week. I suppose I'd been reading about

67

sexuality at college and having more sexual feelings about Kathryn. And I was Catholic, so I went to Confession and I accused myself of impure thoughts. And the priest said, 'You must avoid this. You know they're bad, don't you?' 'Oh yes, father.' But I don't think I knew they were bad. And I have never felt that my feelings for Kathryn were in any way wrong or bad. I just thought perhaps they were impractical. That she wouldn't feel that way about me.

So, in 1969, I'd already arranged that I was coming over to Kathryn when my father died, shortly before I left. And that was all a very nasty business. I had very bad attacks of asthma and was in hospital and my father was in hospital. And I came out and he didn't. It has always been very difficult for me dealing with thoughts about my father, the way he couldn't express his feelings. Perhaps it was all the disappointments of his life that made him like that.

It was strange at first when I moved to London. I found so much to see and television was so astonishing in its criticism of the government. It was really quite a culture shock.

Kathryn and I just lived together till we got the car because, being in a wheelchair I can't use public transport, and getting cabs is very expensive. And she's such a thrifty Scot. So really we just lived together, this sort of closeted couple. We were getting *Sappho* magazine, Kathryn had been getting *Arena Three*, still going then in 1969. She belonged to the MRG and got their newsletter. And we met our first two other lesbian couples. They belonged to CHE and had twice monthly meetings. When I went I found it very friendly and welcoming. I had this wonderful feeling coming into this room full of gay people and I really felt, 'At last I've come home. This is really what I've been waiting for without knowing it.' Suddenly coming into a whole room where everybody was gay.

Through *Sappho* I got in touch with another disabled lesbian. She said she wanted friends who would accept the fact of her disability. We arranged to meet and then she said, 'I think we should find out if there are some other disabled lesbians like us who can't get to these lesbian meetings.' We put a letter in *Sappho* and from that we slowly started to form the group GEMMA. That would be in 1976. We recruited a few of the friends that we'd made at CHE, and she had friends. I hadn't intended to come out through GEMMA. I thought I could be a person just on paper, answering letters and doing the ads. But that was impossible. We'd got lots of other disability groups writing to us or wanting to meet us or wanting an article. And so you really couldn't stay in the background.

In 1977, we were on a TV programme, 'TV Link', but we didn't get a single response. They didn't put our address up on the screen. They said people could write to the TV station and they would forward things on. I just think they had no idea of what it's like for isolated lesbians who are terrified of other people getting hold of their names and addresses and who really needed a direct route to write to.

I think probably we tried to do too much. If we'd just settled to be a penfriend group maybe that would have been better. We've got a quarterly newsletter which contains all the friendship listings and women can write to each other, can be phone friends or can arrange to meet. Quite a few have met their partners through GEMMA, but that's not the chief aim. It really acts as a friendship and support group. We've had letters to GEMMA from women who have separated from their partner or whose partner has died and they've just come into the group and had no other close lesbian friends to talk about it with. The families haven't understood. There's just simply the support we can give each other in forming this network. In London we have a monthly meeting and women in Liverpool and Brighton are trying to organize meetings. Next year will be the tenth year of GEMMA's existence, so I hope that we'll bring out an anthology of work.

I have become Chair of the Employment and Disability Group, to promote employment for disabled people in the Borough of Newham. I'm involved with the British Council of Organizations of Disabled People, a national body formed entirely of groups run by disabled people themselves, because GEMMA was a founding member. I'm also on SPODS Council, that is Sexual and Personal Relationships of Disabled Persons, and we're working on a leaflet specifically for lesbians and gay men with disabilities. I represent GEMMA on the Committee of Newham Associations for Disabled. I'm treasurer and do co-ordinating work for a Dock-lands weekly drop-in for disabled and able-bodied people. And Kathryn and I work with a gay drop-in here in East London, for women and men. We also work with the Gay Vegetarian Group. I hope to continue working with what used to be the Gay Working Party at County Hall.

Kathryn and I have been trying to get more lesbian material on tape. I taped *Tele-woman*, which is a little American journal which has very good personal histories in it from lesbians, about how they grew up, how they realized they were lesbian, and so on. I think a lot more lesbian groups could have accessible meetings and I think a lot of them could make it easier for deaf women to join their groups very often, by speaking more clearly and using finger spelling which you can learn in fifteen minutes. There's also a great need for more information and books in braille and on tape for blind lesbians. Sometimes I think we made a mistake in forming GEMMA, that we should have stayed in *Sappho* and kept pushing at them to organize accessible meetings. But on the other hand, having a sort of lesbian disability group means that we've been able to push other disability groups and say, 'What are you doing about the disabled lesbians and gay men in your group?'

Q: *Looking back in general over your life, what would you say have been the most important influences on you?*

I suppose inevitably one says parents. I keep thinking, my poor mother's not coming very well out of this, but really in an indirect way she was a positive influence. She didn't emphasize femininity. She didn't expect me to keep clean and tidy. I never noticed what I wore, and I think that was quite good because I didn't become very self-conscious and pretentious as a lot of little European girls do in Africa, because femininity is really stressed. I think in some ways it was good that my father was kind of for free speech and freedom of thought, but he was also very restricting and confining in other ways.

I really feel that Kathryn's enabled me to be what I am in all sorts of simple things: being able to be left-wing and to say my own thoughts, which I eventually couldn't do at home. Of course being able to be lesbian. Being a vegetarian has become a very important philosophy with me. I'm now a vegan and I would never have done that without her.

This is our sixteenth year together and they seem to have gone just like that. I think it does get better: you think you won't be getting closer because you're close enough already, but it does get more and more. The other thing about my relationship with Kathryn is that she's able bodied and I'm not. I think a great deal of our relationship is trust. She's accepted everything about me. She's had to do very intimate things for me when I've been ill. Some people have said to me, 'Well, I suppose Kathryn's a nurse.' As if the only woman who could live with a disabled woman is a nurse. And I'd say, 'No, she's had no nursing training whatever.' You see, in that way, I've come to trust her so much.

I can't say that I don't have regrets about my disability. I think, would Kathryn and I be having a much more different life if I weren't disabled. The things I miss with her are silly things I suppose. We've never been able, say, to jump on a bus together. What fun that would be, just to go down the street together or go on the tube. Going off somewhere together is such a safari: getting in the car and getting the wheelchair in.

A woman wrote recently that never before have women had energy and time to work together, and we don't know what, historically, will come out of that. I think we've got this great opportunity. I don't know what will come out of it but, you know, it might be something really wonderful.

I keep thinking to myself, I am so lucky to be a lesbian. I really do see it as great good fortune, to have been born like this, become like this, whatever it is. I wouldn't choose different at all.

POSTSCRIPT

Kathryn and I are still living in London. I continue as co-ordinator of GEMMA, which has grown to about 250 members nationwide. I am also very active as Chair of the Newham (London) Employment and Disability Group, who are in the process of creating and expanding work opportunities for disabled people within the borough; a work centre is to open in spring 1988, a production centre is planned, and co-ops are being set up. There is also extensive liaison with employers on opportunities for the disabled. As well as all this, I'm acquiring computer skills and generally getting into the technological side of things.

Elsa Beckett, March 1988

With Maria in Ronda, Andalucia, Spain, 1986.
Photograph by Sheila Thompson

SUSAN LEIGH

INTERVIEWED ON 7 JULY 1985 BY MARGOT FARNHAM

My father's parents came from Poland in the late nineteenth
century. My grandfather had fled the pogroms, aimed at going to
America but ended up in London in the East End, where he met
my grandmother. All his life he never learnt much English and
managed to run a business and so on by speaking Yiddish the
whole time. He and my grandmother managed to scrape the
money together to start their own tinware business, a little factory
in Hanbury Street. I did see the old account book that my grandmother had kept in beautiful copperplate, and she had done all the
clerical work and all the English-speaking for him. My father took
over the business and during the war the factory thrived. It was
quite unbelievable that we were living in a certain amount of style
and this was all possible because of a dirty, backstreet office, an
antiquated production plant, and at the most about ten workers.

My mother was illegitimate. Her stepfather was a furrier in the
City Road. When she was thirteen or fourteen, my mother was
sent to school in Monaco where she had her first affair at fourteen.
She can remember mixing with the Russian Ballet Company in
the early 1920s. Her stepfather was a total rake, who used to take
her out when she was thirteen or fourteen and then go on the town
and leave her in cafés. Then my mother came to London and
worked as a secretary and became very interested in the thirties
political and literary scene. She had many lovers and two
marriages, but she has told me very little about her ex-husbands.

When she met my father I think she was quite poor and he was
quite well-off and married to a Jewish woman. Seven years later,
my parents were able to get married because my father's divorce

73

came through. She had two children, me and my brother.

I was born during the war in Tring, near Aylesbury, in a comfortable bourgeois home with gardens. And so my earliest memories are of the country, and having a little pony to ride, and woods. And then, when I was five, we moved to London. I was very shocked and I couldn't understand what had happened, because it seemed as though everything had been destroyed. There were all these bomb-sites and I can remember saying to my mother, 'What happened here? Why is it like this?'

We had a house in Hampstead and I hated moving to the city. I had to leave my pony and I hated the idea of change. Because my father had made quite a bit of money they had a butler and a cook, and a nanny for me. My first school was a little private school in Hampstead and that was an enormous shock. My parents decided that, because my mother veered between Catholic and Protestantism in her faith and my father was Jewish but lapsed, this would cause conflict and they shouldn't tell me about the existence of religion. So when I saw everybody praying and talking about the Holy Ghost I was totally mystified, and the teachers were horrified because I said, 'What is this ghost? And why are you all standing with your heads bent over?' They were quite nasty to me and I can remember being really traumatized by suddenly finding that religion existed.

My earliest London memories are of playing in the garden in Hampstead and also of the Great Freeze of 1947. Of course there was rationing at the time and incredible cold, and so there was this big house [laughs] and all these servants and everybody freezing to death because there wasn't coal.

We moved to a large flat by Battersea Bridge in Chelsea, and we still had a nanny who stayed with us right through until my adolescence. I suppose she should be terribly important in my life, because she was there and somebody I talked to a lot, but she isn't at all. It seems awful now, that she was so taken for granted.

Overlapping between Hampstead and Chelsea, my mother decided that I should go to stage school to do ballet and tap and act. I'm never quite sure why she thought I had any talent in this direction. Anyway, I was sent to the Italia Conti stage school, which bred lots of versions of Lena Zavarone, and then the Arts Educational School behind Park Lane. And we did lessons in the morning and ballet and tap and what's called 'character dancing' in the afternoon, which is like folk dancing and you bounce around the room in folk costumes of an indeterminate variety. I suppose it was a lot more fun than going to a straight school. But then my father began to get worried that I wasn't having much of an education, so I was sent to a seedy private school off Eaton Square in Chelsea, run by two older sisters with iron-grey hair.

I went from there to a girls' public day school, the Francis Holland School, behind Sloane Square. Education there in the early fifties seemed to be aimed at turning you into good bourgeois girls who went on to take cordon bleu courses, to finishing schools, or to become up-market secretaries. Few of the girls went to University and the school was badly under-resourced, especially in science equipment. I think I'd have got a much better education at a grammar school or at a boys' public day school. I did have a best friend who was interested in continental films and we thought we were very daring because we had a free-love attitude to sex. My mother's progressive background meant that she was very frank about sex on the whole, although her ideas were very Freudian. You know, I can remember her telling me that clitoral orgasms were no good and a sign of immaturity, which had a lasting and difficult effect on me [laughs].

My mother's view of lesbians was that they were unattractive women who couldn't get a man. Being a girls' public day school, most of the teachers were single women because of the thirties marriage bar, and I'm quite sure a few of them were lesbians. One of them definitely was: our French teacher, who used to wander round in a tailored skirt and jacket, a tie and an Eton crop [laughs]. I don't think there was any doubt at all about her sexuality and I really liked her, but you were brought up to pity her. My mother said, 'poor spinsters'. She always had a couple of little stories about being accosted by lesbians in toilets when she was young, so she gave me this vision of the predatory lesbian, who might jump on me in a toilet! I wasn't exactly given any positive images of lesbians! [laughs].

It was also strange that my mother had gone through all that stuff in the thirties and then married my father and became quite conservative. They both voted Conservative and hated the Attlee government who taxed them. There was that side to my parents which was extremely unlikeable. To try and understand that, there was the Holocaust and the fact that my father's family had two hundred relatives that they knew of around Warsaw and to their knowledge only one survived. I think they did have incredibly strong feelings of insecurity, of having to pass and make it in the world. During the war, my mother didn't live with my father, partly because they thought that one way to survive would be if she didn't appear to be connected to him. Also at school, I was told never to tell anybody I was Jewish.

At one stage I got very involved in religion. I don't think it lasted very long but, being me, I became totally fanatical about it and insisted upon being baptized and confirmed then took communion regularly, very early in the morning. The event which led me to stop believing in religion happened when I was taking communion and I saw the priest's shoes [laughs]. They were these black Oxfords that all vicars wear and I felt terribly annoyed that they should be so unaesthetic and didn't seem to have anything to do with this wonderfully spiritual religion. I just completely lost faith and never went back to church. Also I started to go out with a boyfriend shortly afterwards and I think a lot of my sexual feelings were being sublimated by this religious intensity.

I had my first sexual relationship when I was fourteen with my best friend's brother and we had a sensitive, very romantic, teenage, over-the-top affair and we didn't have penetrative sex which was quite interesting. We went to stay with their grandmother in Jersey. The house was full of pictures of dead pheasants and highland cattle. Their mother was from a Scottish upper-class family and she made her living painting these stately portraits of people's wretched cattle, surrounded by greenery on the estate. Anyway, I was discovered coming out of his room in the morning and the grandmother immediately turned round, took me out for a car ride and said, 'Isn't it a pity you have to leave so soon.' [laughs]. 'I hoped you could stay for longer.'

My mother and father had a very, very stormy relationship. My father had an incredibly violent temper and my mother always says I was the only one who really stood up to him. My mother had pneumonia, and from when I was about twelve she used to live in the Canary Islands for about six months of the year, partly for her health and, as much as anything, to escape my father.

I took my O levels at fifteen and left school early. When I was at this very non-academic school, I think I should have said to my parents that I would go to a tech college and do my A levels there, but I couldn't bear the thought of spending another couple of years at home with my father, with my mother away in the winter, and my parents fighting all summer. What I did say was, 'I'm going to leave school just after my O levels and if you don't let me, I'll leave home anyway and go and work in Woolworth's.' Now I think it really a class-bound, rather snobbish thing to say, but at that time that was my ultimate in rebellion. Because she couldn't think of anything else for me to do, my mother suggested that I go to Paris and learn to be a beautician and enrolled me for this course. I was about sixteen-and-half by then.

The beauty school was the Institut de Beaute de Dr Payot on the Rue de Castiglione. On the first day, I knocked on this imposing door and I was wearing one of these huge, green duster coats from C&As and flat shoes. I never wore any make-up and my hair was in an Italian bubble-cut that was popular in the fifties. And I was ushered in to this room where there was a heavily made-up Russian woman who was probably about seventy-five or could have been eighty. You know, the real stereotype of a madame of a brothel, but she was actually the madame of this beauty school, and she looked at me and she said, 'Oh my God, an English girl!' and she literally said, like in the films, 'Take her away and do something with her!' They put me in one of these beauty chairs and she came along with a huge magnifying glass and peered at my skin and said, 'Oh my God, open pores.' And then they gave me this beauty treatment and made me up in this incredibly exaggerated fifties style so that I felt like a clown. I went back on the metro and couldn't wait to get home and wipe the lot off. At that time, I was living in a small hotel in Montmartre and I'd moved in with a Pakistani student, and he took one look at this incredible face and nearly died.

Fortunately on this course was a young woman from Finland who was very lively and we teamed up and decided to move into a flat together. For many months we lived in these attic rooms you get in hotels for domestic staff and people who are too poor to afford a proper room. The floors were just wood with a little rug and you weren't allowed to cook in your rooms, and of course we did. So we had these illicit paraffin stoves and I can always remember catching light to the floor regularly and stamping out the flames, blue flames running along the floorboards.

We had an enormous amount of fun together, like hitching out of Paris for weekends, and we were both insomniacs so we'd walk around Paris all night. I lived on the smallest amount I possibly could, because I didn't want to ask my father for very much money. We shared places together for about nine months or so and really enjoyed it, and didn't bother with having relationships with men at all most of the time.

One of the political things that struck me about Paris was the Algerian War. I said I was involved with this man who was a Pakistani. Because they looked North African, he and his friends were regularly being rounded up and pulled into police stations. There was a curfew on all Algerians at night. They could round people up and pull them in and thump them about. I was involved with another bloke just before I left Paris who was about to go into the army on his national service. After he left he wrote me a couple of times and said he was horrified at the way they were torturing prisoners. I'm surprised the letters got through.

What I liked about Paris was its beauty, and going to the jazz cellars, and the freedom from home. I also hitch-hiked round Yugoslavia with the Finnish woman long before it got popular with tourists and that was wonderful.

I left Paris in the summer of 1958 and then shared a flat in London with an English woman, Marian, who I'd met in Paris. I told my parents I wanted to earn my own living as a beautician and I used to advertise in *The Times*. I just took three or four clients each week, because I needed very little to live on. During the last few months I was in Paris I'd seen a newsreel about CND nuclear protests going on in England and when I came back to England, I got involved with the Anti-Apartheid Movement and CND immediately. It was quite an exciting time.

I saw this march advertised in the *New Statesman*: 'Demo at So and So'. I went along and about three people turned up and we marched around and then somebody got up on a soapbox and harangued about three individuals and a dog. I later found out they were involved in the Peace League. They were the ones who then told me about the demonstration that was going to take place outside a nuclear plant near Nottingham.

Several thousand people turned up for this demo and the idea was that those who wanted to could invade the site and sit down, and I sat down. I think there was a message from Bertrand Russell, and we were all arrested and carted off to Nottingham

Jail. We spent four days on remand in jail and then my mother heard about it and rushed up with cigarettes and was appalled to see me in prison costume – it was so inelegant – and that was her biggest thing. You know [laughs], the dress is so unbecoming!

I can remember the details of the prison vividly because I felt how terrible it was for the women who have to stay. I was all right because for me it was just a few days. They take away all your clothing and put you in prison clothing which is all cotton and this was mid-winter. And you were locked in your cell for vast lengths of time. I was aware that there were lesbians there, because there were women shouting from cell to cell, 'Sadie, I love you!' or 'Mary, I love you!' While I was there I did hear one woman being dragged screaming into a punishment cell. I think most of us were from middle-class homes and had had no experience of how deeply shocking the conditions were for those women.

I was also quite involved when the French let off their first nuclear bomb. It was amazing how fast people mobilized for that: thousands of people congregated outside the French Embassy and demonstrated all night directly the news came out. Marian and I had a basement flat in Knightsbridge at the time, which was near the Embassy, so for a whole weekend we had all these people lying asleep on the floor or having tea or using it as a general office, so we didn't sleep for about three days.

I'd also heard about the Anti-Apartheid Movement. I had very strong feelings about race, I think to do with being brought up very anti-fascist because of the Holocaust, and what I'd seen happening in Paris around the Algerian War. On the other hand, I had very little political theory. It was very much a gut thing, to do with, 'That is right, and that is wrong.' I'd been along to a few Anti-Apartheid meetings and they were talking about having a boycott of South African goods. Then, when I was at an anti-nuclear meeting, news of Sharpeville was announced and appeals were made to go down to South Africa House, so I went rushing down there. It was decided that there would be a 24-hours-a-day, four-day vigil, in memory of the people who had died. Because I was a beautician and could please myself, I went all night every night and sometimes during the day because big demonstrations were happening as well. There were quite a lot of Black people on the demo, because it was to do with race, and the police were much more violent than on anti-nuclear demos. I can remember

79

Aged 8 (looking up)

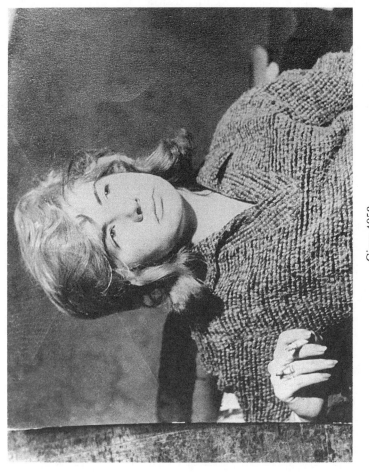

Circa 1958

charging with a load of people and the humiliation of being picked up bodily by this policeman and carried back across the road.

Perhaps I should say something about my husband. I met him on a CND march and he was from a working-class background. My mother was always introducing me to middle-class twits and he seemed a lot more interesting than all of them. I did become infatuated by him, but I also got pregnant. That precipitated me into marriage. When my mother found out I was pregnant, she said that it would be a good idea if I had an abortion, but when I actually got to the place I couldn't go through with it. It was an extraordinary experience. I was taken to a house in a leafy suburb and there were two men, a woman nurse, an ether pad and various instruments. I'd actually got onto the table and I sat up and said, 'No, no, no!' and refused to have it because I had thought that I'd be properly anaesthetized. And they were terribly rude to me, and said, 'Oh you silly girl', and, 'We'll take your money, anyway.'

I got back to my mother, who was not very pleased at the prospect of becoming a grandmother, but I suddenly wanted the baby desperately after that and so then I rang my boyfriend and he said 'I'll marry you', as they did in those days. My parents actually did then say, 'Are you sure you don't want to just live with him?' But I thought, I will marry him. And of course they were horrified because he was working class.

It's awful now, thinking back on it, but I think I was attracted to the idea of living in a working-class way. In view of the guilt I felt about my upbringing and affluence, it seemed to be the fitting thing to do. My husband was working in Chatham in the naval dockyard as an apprentice fitter and we were incredibly poor. We rented a house in Gillingham with a little alley down the back and no hot water and an outside loo. I wanted to have my baby in hospital in London. In those days women were treated abominably. It was that whole dehumanizing thing of being stripped of your clothing, put in a nightie, shaved, given an enema. I wasn't yet nineteen. I was absolutely terrified by the whole process and I had been quite relaxed about it because I thought I'd read all these books and was reasonably well-informed. It was a very easy labour, but unfortunately the hospital was so understaffed that they cut me totally unnecessarily in order to hasten the birth, and the stitches were very clumsily done. Having had a totally painless childbirth, I then passed out at the pain of being stitched up. I never felt I owned my body for years afterwards.

Directly I had given birth to my first baby I was overwhelmed with a feeling of guilt. You know, you are supposed to feel these wonderful happy feelings and I thought, 'Oh gosh, she's come into the world and she's crying already. What have I done? Oh, God, another suffering soul in the world' [laughs]. I had the baby and came back and was suddenly faced with a squalling, puking infant. I thought the baby was really beautiful and I actually liked breastfeeding quite a lot because that was very sensual, and I got very absorbed in the baby and less and less absorbed in my husband, who seemed totally superfluous. I went very much off sex, partly through fear of having another baby and also because I think a baby just takes all your energy.

We moved to a small housing estate, because my husband got offered a job in Wantage, and that was an awful experience for me because I'd always been used to going out to London and suddenly I was on this small town estate where everybody was Mrs Clean. We were on a near starvation income and this was the 'affluent sixties'. On this housing estate, I then had two more babies, at home, which was preferable.

You are totally isolated from any kind of politics in a small town. I couldn't afford evening classes. With small children you can't do any jobs to make any money. My husband was studying on day release and at night school and gave absolutely no help at all. He loved having fun with the children but he never got up in the night because he always said he needed his sleep. I became incredibly resentful. There were sexual pressures too. I also felt guilty because you weren't supposed to feel like that, so all the outrageous behaviour in my husband I excused.

A couple of years after the birth of my third daughter, my husband was offered an army post as a civilian and we moved to an army camp block of flats outside Dusseldorf in Germany. It was an amazing experience because I was suddenly faced with the very active social life of Privates' and Non Commissioned Officers' wives. The army was a shock to me. Of course I was aware of class but in the army there'd be two different doctor's waiting rooms for Officers' wives and Other Ranks' wives. And a circular came round for a dance which said, 'Officers and their ladies,

NCOs and their wives, Other Ranks and their women!' This was 1967. Army wives also have to put up with their husbands being sent on manoeuvres for weeks at a time. You know, because of the pressures on them, the women often had terrible rows, which sometimes led to physical fights, but there was also support and strong friendships between women.

While I was out there, 1968 was happening, without me! I was most interested in the reports of the early Women's Movement. All the media coverage was hostile and sensationalist and about bra-burning, but I can remember thinking, 'Oh, burning your bra – great!' It had a really good effect on me. I thought it all sounded very attractive.

When we got back to England, we settled in Melksham in Wilt-shire. The nearest women's group that I could find was in Chip-penham. I saw a little advert for it outside the Town Hall. There were only two lesbians in the group. I thought they were amazing [laughs] and they were incredibly generous about offering their house for meetings on all days of the week. Their house was taken over by the group, because everybody else was married. At one time there were forty women in that group, and there were lots of little groups, like consciousness-raising, health, and a National Abortion Campaign group. They were almost entirely middle-class, well-educated, white women, mostly in their mid-twenties with young children. They had read about feminist ideas and become very interested in feminism and women's rights. Their husbands were in middle-class jobs. They were all much better off than I was and wore Laura Ashley clothes. This would be 1972 by then.

The CR group I was in was very good. We kept it a closed group. I think there was six of us and we very rarely had any absentees. Each session we explored one area of our lives. We met weekly, and on alternate weeks we discussed the politics of the issue that we'd discussed the week before. We had a lot of laughter as well.

We hardly discussed lesbians at all, which, looking back, was a terrible insult to the two lesbians in the group. We didn't discuss sex that much. I've talked to another woman who was in a similar group and both of us came to the conclusion that probably it was such a dangerous area because we all felt so close and fancied each other! [laughs] There was the whole thing of suddenly getting close to women physically because we all hugged each other a lot, and held hands.

At home, there was the incredible conflict of me saying, 'I will never iron your shirts again', and, 'I want and I will . . . ' This was quite a shock to the old shit-bag who was having a relationship with a woman and hardly living at home. I was also having quite a nice time with my daughters and by this time I'd done A levels and started University. Anyway, all that was going on and then the Chippenham group fell apart; I think we'd gone so far, especially the CR group. And we held the South West Conference at Chippenham. We set up a day conference there and I'd written a paper called 'Dealing with the contradictions in our lives' [laughs] in which I said, 'We've all said that coping with domesticity and our husbands and marriages is difficult, and we have this theory which says that this is against our principles, so why are we doing this? How do we deal with these contradictions?' And there was dead silence and this woman said to me, 'Well, when are you going to pack your bags, Sue?'

I was at college at this point. I went and took my A levels parttime at Chippenham Technical College at the same time working in supermarkets, and then was accepted for University and did a three-year degree course in Sociology at Bristol. I went in 1974, so my children were still quite young and they had to be incredibly self-sufficient. Going to University got my thoughts in order and gave me access to ideas. It was like what women mature students always say, you're doing something entirely for yourself.

When I was working in the supermarket, in 1972, I joined the local Labour Party. Because of what I'd encountered on the army camp about class, I was determined that I would be involved in socialist politics when I returned. I became Political Education Officer while I was doing my degree and became involved in the Westbury Constituency Labour Party, which was being taken over by left-wing intellectual college lecturers who were quite strong on issues like abortion. The year I graduated I supported Grunwick a lot on the mass picket.

During the last year of my degree course, my husband had suddenly started to frequent home a lot and he suddenly said, 'Oh, the children are growing up, won't it be nice, because we'll have lots of time together', and I thought, 'With you?' Even when the children were very small I used to have housewives' daydreams about suddenly walking out and being a completely free woman. I'd realized that children grow up and that things could change. It was 1977 and the unemployment situation had started to escalate. It was very difficult to get a job in Wiltshire with a sociology degree, so I worked in a cream laboratory, then as a Care Officer with the mentally handicapped, so I was doing shit work, and then, luckily, my ex-lecturer offered me some part-time teaching at Chippenham Tech.

My husband was driving me to the limits. He'd started harassing me sexually and staged a sort of nervous breakdown. He would keep me awake all night and then he'd sleep all day. I was mentally in a pretty desperate state and my husband also raped me twice before I left. The children were not as old as I would have wished them to be for me to walk out, but I thought, 'I'll have to go.' First I said to him, 'I want you to leave.' And he said, 'Oh, I cannot go and live in a bedsit, and I won't leave, anyway.' So I contacted the housing co-op in Bath which had just started up and I explained that I was fleeing the marital home and had to get out fast. I got a room in a beautiful house and I was due to move into this house in six weeks' time.

The co-op didn't know that I hadn't yet told my husband or family, and rang up: an absolute shock for the girls. I said to my daughters, 'Look, I really have to go and I can't take you with me and I need to be on my own', and, 'I hope you'll come and see me', and, 'I'll still be around.' My husband kept saying that he was going to kill himself, which the children met with hollow laughter and said, 'When?' with eager voices, and it must have been horrendous for them. While I was waiting for the Bath co-op house to come up, a friend offered me a room in her house.

When I was able to take this room I took a couple of rucksacks of clothes and said goodbye and got on the bus, and I just had this enormous feeling of relief and elation. I was wound up about leaving, especially my youngest daughter, but it was just so wonderful: I didn't have to prepare anybody's meals and I woke up every morning with this feeling of intense excitement and joy, and wandered round Bath endlessly and through the night. It was amazing and some of that has still stayed with me seven years later.

Politically, I'd already joined the NAC group in Bath. I ran a couple of Workers' Education Courses and went to women's conferences. I also made friends with a Dutch lesbian who lived in the same house and, when she went to Holland, I visited her and met lots of Dutch lesbians. I was also working voluntarily in the local community bookshop. I joined the Socialist Workers' Party, briefly. The group actually broke up because of the sexual politics of one of the men: he behaved very badly towards one of the women.

Q: *Can you say something about your coming-out?*

After I left my husband, I'd got more and more interested in women's issues and closer and more attracted to women and I started to read about lesbian sexuality. I found that it all seemed to make sense in terms of my body and my attractions. But I was celibate for about eight months because I wanted to think about it. And I was going to Holland for holidays to see my friend there, and a young woman fell in love with me and said she wanted to sleep with me. And I slept with her and it was wonderful. And that was it. I just felt that it was absolutely natural and what I'd been looking for. It seemed so right. Straight away, I thought, that's it. I'm a lesbian and that's what I've always been.

After that I moved to London to do a course at Goldsmiths' College. I lived in a lesbian house, met more lesbians, joined WAVAW (Women Against Violence Against Women) and a South London Lesbian Group. I've been involved now with an Australian woman, Maria, for nearly five years. It started off as quite a light relationship and has become very strong and very important.

Looking back, I think all my close friendships were with women but I wouldn't say there was this strong, sexual thing, because it was just so deeply buried. It must have been there because I'm so overwhelmed by women. I also think that when I travel, I tend to look at people a lot and watch crowds passing and I suddenly realized that I'd been watching women and children; I never watched men and I was always interested in women's hair and the turn of their necks, which are very beautiful.

POSTSCRIPT

During my second year in London, I became increasingly

depressed about the political situation. The campaigns set up in opposition to Thatcherism lacked imagination and were based on outworn methods which provided safe avenues of protest.

The Women's Movement, though still strong, also seemed to lack energy, through constantly having to defend basic rights. The Women's Movement has always been based on changing ourselves as one way of changing the world. This has meant challenging our own racism and classism. The debates continue to be necessary but take a lot out of us. Many women have retreated into individual solutions: therapy, spirituality, a good job, a nice house. Some women, of course, are able to combine these things with political action, but for many they provide an alternative to politics.

My personal solution to the frustration I felt at not finding anything worthwhile to do politically was to move countries. I've never felt particularly attached to Britain, partly because of my own mixed background and partly because I believe in the saying, 'As a woman I have no country . . . ' Maria and I went to Spain for two years.

We hoped to rent a place for women who wanted a holiday in the sun. It was a gamble as we had no capital. I actually ended up teaching English in Ronda, a small town in Andalusia, where we got the chance to run a vegetarian café for a local rich boy. He had the property; we had the energy and we split the profits.

The restaurant attracted women travelling without men and groups of Spanish women who wanted to meet up in a hassle-free atmosphere. We learnt a lot about tourism, running a foreign business and the politics of food. We never felt isolated as we practically always had friends visiting. We also got a lot of support and friendship from the local community.

Unfortunately, half-way through our second season our patron, seeing the restaurant's great success, managed to throw us out and take it over for himself. We were shattered at the time and still miss the restaurant and Ronda.

We came back to England shocked and without much money. England seemed dirtier, poorer and sadder than ever, except for the rich. We spent the winter of '87–'88 working and saving. We had decided to go back to Maria's homeland, Australia.

In December the Thatcher Government came up with Clause 28 of the Local Government Bill and we joined the Stop the Clause

Campaign. There has been a great response to the clause from lesbians and gay men, many of whom have never been involved in anything political before and it would be wonderful if this energy is sustained.

I also consolidated my friendships with my three daughters who are very supportive of my sexuality. They are quite all right about my going to Australia but I am apprehensive about leaving close friends.

The flipside to this is that I like being a travelling lesbian. By joining political actions as I meet them on my travels I can make an attempt to reconcile my political energy with my restlessness. Interviewed a year from now, I imagine the situation could be completely different.

Susan Leigh, Sydney, March 1988

Hackney, London, 1987. Portrait by Nicky West

GILLI SALVAT

INTERVIEWED ON 29 JUNE 1986 BY ALLEGRA DAMJI

My father was born in 1906 near Calcutta. His father was an Indian railways guard and so he was born in an up country railway station called Raj Mahal in Bihar. My grandfather is said to have been born on an immigrant ship which sailed from Hincklesham in Suffolk to Australia. When he was fourteen he ran away to sea on the tea clippers and landed up in India because Calcutta was a big port for the Raj.

My father was one of three brothers and three sisters and they were all sent to an Indian railways school near a beautiful place called Rishikish at the source of the Ganges. It was run like an English public school – lots of discipline and not much food – and he learnt to shoot, ride and play rugby. He was brought up really hard but I don't think he was like that at all. He came first in his exams out of the whole district and won a chance to go to Cambridge which was very unusual for a working-class boy. But he decided not to go, probably through lack of money.

He met my mother in a town called Digboy when he was twenty-seven and she was seventeen. He was sitting with a friend on the veranda and when he saw my mum he said, 'I'm going to go out with her.' Because he was a bit silver-tongued. On the first date he asked her to marry him. It meant giving up his job because he was passing as a European working in the oil business and had signed a contract forbidding bachelors to marry.

My mum was brought up in a village in Assam, near the border of what is now Bangladesh. Her father was a Scottish tea planter who lived with her mother for three or four years. He sounds like a bastard. He had to leave because he killed one of the labourers

91

on the plantation. Anyway, because my mum was a white man's child, her mother decided to give her an English education, and she was given to a missionary to be looked after. They were all Christian converts as the missionaries were well away up there. When she was twelve she was sent to a famous school called Dr Graham's Colonial Homes, which is now called Kallinpong School. It was set up for Anglo-Indian kids who were being abandoned because they symbolized the taboo of black and white sex and illegitimacy. She left school to become a nanny, and that's what she was doing when she met my dad.

I was born in 1942, in the middle of the war, when my father was on active service. The British called him up rather than his brothers and I think it had something to do with his fair skin and his cleverness. He was a captain in the Royal Indian Army Corps that was stationed at the Northwest Frontier. In India – unless you had money, in which case there would be no barriers – your class depended on the colour of your skin. It was stratified, according to caste with the Hindus, and colour with the British.

After the war my father took us to Calcutta because there was more work there. My father was a drunk. In colonial countries the men of the mixed race community often abuse alcohol. He used to go on binges where he would disappear for a week or two and then return absolutely ravaged and worry my mum for money. He nearly died once through drinking by bursting a large blood vessel in his intestines, and I remember a doctor coming in the middle of the night because he'd tried to do himself in by drinking a bottle of iodine. He was really desperate and now he might have been helped but then he was just a drunk. He still held down a job, though, because he was clever and a wonderful liar.

My parents sent me and my older sister to this posh convent school run by Carmelite nuns, because they wanted us to have a good education. I hated it because it was so restrictive and because I was affected by what was going on at home to the extent that I could hardly read and write until I was about eight. My mum also had five abortions because they couldn't afford to have any more children and she was worried my dad would drop dead any minute. She said I was allowed to live because I was conceived during the war during one of their leaves and I was their 'love child' [chuckles]. But when my dad wasn't drunk he was lovely, and potty about the family. I was very close to my mum. I slept with her until I was about six and I just wouldn't leave her side. I think I was used as a form of contraception as well.

A lot was happening in India at the time. Independence Day came and I remember in 1947 when the Union Jack came down at school and the Indian flag went up and we sang the Indian national anthem for the first time and everyone was crying. Calcutta is a very raw city. Naked fakirs used to sit outside our house covered in ashes and with garlands round their necks. That's been banned now. And there was a beggar woman who would come round every fortnight and have an epileptic fit in front of the house and she'd always have a different new-born baby in her arms which would go flying. There was a fakir with a tin box on his head who used to appear with two wives; one played a drum and the other had a whip. And the guy would go whirling round and round and one woman would drum and the other would whip him and he'd go faster and faster until eventually he'd collapse and go into a religious trance. Then the two women would open the box but I never saw what was in it [laughs]. All these scenes from my childhood are very powerful.

After Independence an Indianization Programme was set in motion. The Anglo-Indians had key institutional jobs – telephones, electric, water and the railways – and the Indian government wanted to reclaim those sort of jobs. It meant my parents' lifestyle, such as it was, was being threatened. My mother had heard about the Welfare State through the BBC World Service, and she knew my father was unstable so she thought we should go to England while we could. If you live in a place with no Welfare State there is no limit to how far you can fall. We got into England for two reasons; one, my dad had been an officer in the British Army and, two, the 'Grandfather Clause' which meant that because his father was born on a British ship he was considered British. We got a P&O liner from Bombay and I remember standing on the rail of the boat as it pulled away from India. That night my parents were crying and crying and India was getting smaller and smaller and all the lights were getting dimmer and dimmer, and I didn't really understand why they were crying. They were crying because they would never see her again.

The boat had come from Sydney: they used to do a run, Australia, India, Aden, and through the Suez Canal to England.

We went first class because of a booking cancellation. The Colonial Office had paid our passage and my dad was still paying them back when he died fourteen years later. I remember going into a lounge where these white Australians were at the next table, and when we sat down they said, 'What are these wogs doing in here?' My dad made us get up and walk out and that was my first experience of white prejudice. I knew he wanted to kill them.

I remember when we were going through the Suez Canal the Captain announced that all ladies were to go to their cabins but my mum peeped out of her cabin window and saw that as the boat was going through all these Egyptian guys used to lift up their jellabas and flash [laughs].

When we docked at Tilbury we were taken to an immigrant hostel at the basement of a church near Selfridges. Men and women were separated and we slept on these iron cots. My dad walked all over London looking for a place for us to live, but nobody wanted coloureds or children. The only shop we knew about was Harrods because it was famous throughout the Empire, and so they took us there to buy my sister and I overcoats because we had no warm clothing. People were so unused to seeing Asian people they used to stop in their tracks and stare at us down Oxford Street. We were there for a few months and then the truant officer came and told my parents they had to send us to school. The nearest was St George's of Hanover Square, which was for all these posh kids from Mayfair. They were really racist to me. They used to pick on me all the time and I remember coming from a terrible day at school to sleep in these iron cots with people who were coughing and crying.

Eventually my dad found us some rooms in Mill Hill owned by a widow. My parents found her really dirty. She used to sleep with her dog and in India that is unbelievable. All of us used to have a bath every day because that's what you do in India but this was the fifties and things were still on ration, and here she was with these lodgers using up all the hot water [laughs]. I think it's called 'cultural conflict'. She gave us notice after eight months and we found a two-bedroomed flat in Hendon. My mum still lives there. I was sent to a council school which was a great contrast to the one in Mayfair, but they took the piss equally as much, because of how I talked. And I think in about three weeks I changed my accent and I started learning to survive. I began to hit people if they said things to me: I became a lot happier and gained some respect. I also started to learn how to read and write. School in England was a lot freer and I liked that.

A lot of women started going out to work in the fifties and, because we couldn't live on my father's wages, my mum got a job in a factory making brass plates. My father had good exams and work experience but this didn't count for anything because he came from India. He got work as a low grade clerk. But he did not want his wife to go out to work: it was a real challenge to his manhood. On one level he was really into my mum but on another he would really demean her. He was always saying she was 'stupid' or 'couldn't do anything'. She didn't have any confidence in herself and, when she got a full-time job, he started drinking again. I don't know how my mum took it. She had to be at work at eight o'clock in the morning and do piecework on a machine as big as a house, *and* deal with my dad, who was in a terrible state. It was a hard time and my school work suffered because of it. When it came to taking the eleven plus I failed dismally and went to Secondary Modern. From about thirteen I started catching up. In my second year I came top of the class and that really pleased me and my parents. It was a critical time to do it because it meant I went on to learn shorthand and typing in the next year instead of needlework.

There was no sex education at school or at home. When I first started menstruating my mother completely freaked out. I was sitting on the kitchen table and I found blood on my knickers. 'Get off the table, you'll get blood all over the table cloth', she said and I felt really frightened. Blokes didn't fancy me at school. I was too stroppy and all the ideal girls were blonde-haired and blue-eyed. But I was very popular with the girls. I was a gang leader. I used to get a girls' comic called *School Friend* – all the girls' comics were about secrets, things like *The Silent Three* – you know, all these middle-class white girls at boarding school with hoods and masks. I had a good time at school really.

This was the late fifties and a coffee bar opened up in our area. It was incredible, all these hip young people used to go there. Me and my friend were the youngest and we used to just sit there with an espresso and stare at everyone. It was at that time that I fell in love with rock'n'roll from the time I heard my first record. It had such an impact on my life: I was just never the same again. You only know what it was like if you knew what music was like before. I was mad about Elvis, Bill Haley, Fats Dominoe, and Little Richard because they were rebels and were saying something special to young people. American culture in general – books and music – was a big influence on my life. The only way Indian culture was kept alive was through my parents speaking Hindi to each other. I would never have thought to learn it myself but I understood everything they talked about. My mum somehow kept our culture alive with food and language and all the stories from the past.

My first lesbian relationship was with a girl in my gang. She was the prettiest girl in the class. She also had a ponytail [laughs] and we fell in love. We used to sit in her room kissing and cuddling and being very intense with each other. And one day I arrived at her house to find her really upset and she told me her mum had found her diary and had banned her from seeing me for the rest of the summer. I was so naive I didn't know what was going on. So I said, 'Show me your diary' and I got it out from under her bed and read it and for the past few weeks on practically every page she'd written that she loved me and wanted to be with me. I was absolutely astounded, because it was what I felt as well but she'd actually articulated it.

So I spent quite a lonely summer without her. We hadn't heard of the word lesbian, homosexual, gay, nothing. I didn't know anything about it but somewhere inside of me, and because of her parents' reactions, I knew there was something wrong. Her parents started encouraging her to go out with boys and she had plenty after her. There I was, knowing she loved me, but not being able to go near her; it was really painful. This situation went on for about two years.

I only bunked off once in my life and that was to be with Ann. We went back to my parents' flat because I knew they'd be at work. It was one of the few times we got into bed together and we were really getting into it. It was just so exciting we were almost fainting and suddenly there was this knocking on the door. Luckily I'd bolted the door and it was a flat with no back door, but it had a fire escape. It was my mum, and we were in bed together! *Naked!* It was my poor mum and she'd come home from work ill and couldn't get the door open, and she was crying and calling my name. I got Ann and pushed her half-dressed up the fire escape. Meanwhile my mum had come back with the caretaker and somehow I'd worked out this plan and when they knocked again I opened it and said, 'Oh, it's you!' and she said, 'What on earth is going on?'. So I made up this story about being ill and having to come home from school and she believed me, but I still had to work out how to get Ann down from the roof. So it's getting on for lunchtime and I said I wanted to go back to school and my mum said, 'Oh, don't be silly, it's all right, I'll look after you.' So I had to make up all this bullshit, get me school clothes on, go down the stairs, walk down the street so she saw me, then double back and creep up to the roof to let Ann out. She was completely freaked out and crying, and I had to shut her up to get her past the front door.

All these things affected the way I felt about that relationship. Everything screamed at me that it was wrong, though there was nothing down in print. Finally when she was fifteen or so she broke away from me and within a year she'd left school and married this Malaysian bloke who looked like me. That was the last I saw of her, though I know she was divorced within two years, and I still regret how much I pushed her away because of my own fear.

I left school at sixteen and got a job with the British Council as a trainee shorthand typist. It was a great place to work because I met people from all over the world. I also started getting interested in politics: the Civil Rights Movement in America and Sharpeville in South Africa had a particularly strong impact. As I was growing up I identified with the underdog because I felt like an underdog.

At that time my one ambition was to go to college. No, I had two ambitions, one, I wanted . . . I had three ambitions [laughs]. One, I wanted to find someone to love; two, I wanted to see the world, and three, I wanted to go to college. Anyway, one day I went into a jazz record shop on the Charing Cross Road and there was this wonderful record playing. So I asked the bloke behind the counter who it was by and he got red and said, 'Actually, it's my record. I just recorded it in Germany.' I got embarrassed and left and he followed me and asked me if I wanted to go for a cup of coffee. And that was Mr Salvat.

Mr Salvat was wonderful, my hero. He was thirty and I was

seventeen. He'd lived all over the world – Africa, Asia, Europe. On the Saturday after we'd met it was my parents' Silver Anniversary, and they were having a party and in the middle of it – knock, knock – who should be at the door but Mr Salvat. My father took an instant dislike to him because he was an older man and my mum loved him [laughs]. But Maurice, that's his name, wanted me and that was it. On our second date he asked me to marry him at Hendon Central Tube and I just laughed and he said, 'What are you laughing at? I've never asked anybody else in my life to marry them', and I said 'Don't be stupid – you hardly know me', and he said, 'You'll find out that I'm sincere.' He asked me practically every time we met after that. We started going out in November and by February I was head over heels in love and wanted to marry him too.

We spent a lot of time in bed together but not screwing, because I was a virgin and I'd said I didn't want him to do it with me, I don't know how he managed, but he did and it just got deeper and deeper. As it came nearer to our wedding we started to fuck and it was amazing. I'd never felt turned on like that except with Ann. A lot of women have bad times with men sexually, but it wasn't like that for me. He was really ill though and had just had a tumour removed from his testicle, and we had to ask his surgeon if it was okay for us to marry. We also had to get my parents' consent, as the age of majority was then twenty-one and they were reluctant to give it because they were frightened for me. But they could see I was mad about him so eventually we got married.

He introduced me to a whole new world. His parents were French and he'd been living in Germany but he'd come to England to establish himself on the jazz circuit and we lived in a one-room flat in Earls Court. All his friends were people from the jazz world that I'd heard about as a fan and now here I was sitting around their houses. I was absolutely entranced. I used to sit looking pretty and listening; I didn't have a thing to say myself. We moved in with Ginger Baker and his wife and we became very good friends, and it was while we were there that Maurice died of a cerebral haemorrhage.

I was absolutely devastated. I was a widow at twenty-one. I remember saying to my dad, 'Please, please help me, you've got to do all this for me because I can't.' And he just put his arm round me and said, 'Don't worry. I'll do everything.' And I can't remember those weeks: it is completely blocked out. I don't know how I coped. My dad got the funeral together and about three weeks after I got a job and it was the right thing to do. I stayed and faced it on the advice of my sister. I had wanted to run away but I'm glad I stayed. Three months later my father decided to end his life.

I started working in one of the most successful music agencies of the sixties, called the Tito Burns Agency. It had all the big stars of the sixties. They handled Dusty Springfield, Dionne Warwick, the Searchers, Bob Dylan, Burt Bacharach, Kiki Dee, and Joan Baez, and I was meeting all these people. It was great but I didn't like the commercialism of the music industry. I wasn't happy at the time either. And then I met a man called Stevie. He was very pretty and he came from a Hungarian–Jewish background and I suppose I fell for him. It wasn't anything like my husband, but we got on really well and learnt a lot together.

In 1968 Stevie and I went overland to India. We were influenced by the hippie movement, though we couldn't drop out as we had to earn a living, but we were into the whole ideological, philosophical and political alternative society. It was very exciting: I loved the sixties. There wasn't really a Black movement in Britain then, so I suppose going to India was for me like regaining my roots; but I hadn't read anything saying those things then. When I walked across the Indian border from Pakistan I just burst out crying and I thought, 'I'm coming home.' The last time I'd seen it was on the boat with my parents crying. Every single day in India taught me something new. I went back to Calcutta to the street where we lived and I met people and family that had known my parents. When we came back we were practically starving because we'd run out of money while there. And then I said that I wouldn't be able to go back to India for another ten years because it was a devastating experience. India made me feel proud of being Indian, or it consolidated that for me.

In the meantime Ginger Baker and his wife had got very rich and famous and they were going to do a tour of the States. They asked me to come along to look after their kids. So there I was on tour with The Cream, a mega-group of the sixties. It was amazing seeing the United States from a first-class angle, after all the American books I'd read. When I came back I started a craft business at some of the markets around Portobello Road and

Mother, father and sister in India

1965

At 15

Marriage 1961

Aged 2, in Bombay

Bayswater with Stevie. We just couldn't work in conventional jobs any more [laughs]. At this time there was only one video machine in the whole country and it belonged to John Lennon. Stevie got involved in making agitprop video with this sixties figure called Hoppy.

My first adult lesbian relationship was with Hoppy's girlfriend. I was twenty-nine and she was about twenty-five. She was very beautiful, clever, and neurotic. I had never met anyone like her before. She gave me a really hard time. I was obsessed with her and I used to share her with Hoppy. He used to come out of her room and I'd be waiting to go in: that sort of scene. It got to the stage where I was either going to top myself or I was going to get out of it, so I got out. Even though it was so negative in some ways, after that, I knew that I wanted to be with women.

The relationship with Stevie was on the rocks because I was getting more independent. He also wanted to get involved with my relationships with women, and my emerging feminism was making me very angry about that. It was about that time that I started doing youth work. I worked two nights a week at this club in Paddington for sort of pre-skinhead white kids who were into pills and alcohol. So I was doing very commercial work in the music and advertising business and then working in a youth club and getting off with women. I started doing this part-time youth work course and one of the youth officers said why didn't I do a full-time course at college. I never thought anybody would say that to me and I thought, 'Why not?' At last I felt right doing something. So after a lot of persuasion from friends I applied for the Youth and Community Course at Goldsmiths' College. Five hundred people applied and there was twenty-five places and I got in! I was over the moon but very frightened too.

I can't tell you what an enormous place Goldsmiths' had to play in my life. I found my voice there and I haven't stopped talking since. I'd been around all these creative people and I'd spent a lot of my life listening, pleasing, and servicing, but that was changing. I was the first Asian student at Goldsmiths' and there are still very few of us that have Youth and Community Work diplomas, and I was an out lesbian which was very unusual then. I took some stick at that college and almost didn't make it in the end. My community politics really developed through placements like the NCCL Gay Rights Committee and The Joint Council for the Welfare of Immigrants.

I also had a placement for two years working with the Bengali community in Brick Lane. I was totally engrossed in learning as much as I could. I started going out with an American woman called Carol Lee, who was one of the lesbians who fought for the sixth demand of the Women's Movement. She was the one who taught me about being a lesbian. She taught me how to make love [laughs] and sorted my politics out. I'd been sleeping with straight and bisexual women up till then and she was the first real lesbian that I had a relationship with. She taught me so much.

When I finished college I got a job as a Senior Youth Worker at Caxton House which is a very big community centre in Archway. I was employed to set up the youth provision there. That was when Carol Lee started to go off me. She wanted me to live with her in Brighton and when I got the job she knew I wasn't going to. I'd just got myself an education. She was a highly-educated person and there was no way I was going to say, 'I'm going to drop this' and ride off into the sunset to support yet another person to realize their genius.

From the beginning the job was very heavy. The catchment area was old council estates in the process of being knocked down to make way for new ones and all the streets around were tinned up. The majority of the young people who came to the centre were Afro-Caribbean young men. There was hardly any women youth workers. Out of 356 workers in the ILEA youth section only sixty were women, and of those I was one of the few with a senior position. We were under a lot of pressure, so some of us decided to set up a group. We met at A Woman's Place and there was five or six of us, and within three months there was forty or fifty of us meeting there because we were all having such a bad time at work. I had a male assistant and my management committee and the young people would only refer to him. We were all getting stick and we decided to come together to struggle and it resulted in the first real feminist input into youth work. And me and a friend – called Val, who had been at Goldsmiths' with me – set up the two first Girls' Nights in our clubs in the whole of London. They were the first feminist, non-uniform, non-religious girls' nights doing non-traditional activities.

It was hard. My life was threatened by some of the young men in the club, who were so hostile to the girls' night that they attacked the woman football coach. We had started a women's football league as a way of getting girls together. After that incident I had to ban four of the boys and from that moment they were after me. After weeks of intimidation I decided to turn male violence against male violence and I employed this guy called Delroy, a Rasta security guard, to protect me. In fact Delroy didn't have to be violent. He had such a dread image that he just had to stand there and he sorted the whole thing out and defused it.

Our work with young women grew and developed. In Camden and Islington I was lucky enough to be in touch with a group of feminist youth workers who were as equally committed to getting young women a good deal in the Youth Service as I was. Louie, my girlfriend, was one of these women and was involved with me in running the Girls' Night at Caxton House. The group of us were very close and at times it was euphoric the way we worked together to make things happen. We experimented with all kinds of activities for young women (some of them borrowed from our experience in the Women's Movement) like a young women's disco, discussion groups, non-traditional sport, arts and crafts. Because of our contact with young women, knowing that they were hungry for all kinds of new activities and experiences, we started to pressure the ILEA hierarchy to set up specialized young women's projects which would cater for their particular needs.

Eventually in 1979 with the help of local women, the first two full-time girls' projects – one in Camden and one in Islington – were set up, after many a committee meeting, argument, and even a picket of the London Youth Committee in County Hall. I was lucky enough to get the job in Islington and my old pal Jane Dixon the one in Camden. We were all innovators and pioneers in our field and, seven years on, it's been wonderful to see how things have grown and blossomed. There is now a National Organization for Work with Young Women, which links young women and women youth workers from Scotland to Cornwall, and literally hundreds of groups up and down the country.

One of the ways we worked was to use our own skills and experiences to match the needs of the young women we were working with. So I tried to set up facilities for two groups of young women who were nearest to my heart: lesbians and Asian young women. Dixie and I started working with the Young Lesbian Group almost as soon as we started work at the Girls' Projects.

This was because a group of lesbians who were meeting at the mixed London Gay Teenage Group wanted to break away and meet on their own. No one had ever done youth work with young lesbians before, so it was all highly controversial. We were taking a hell of a risk with everything we did so we had to work very carefully and strictly, but it was a wonderful experience. For the first time as youth workers we could be entirely 'out' and feel that we were truly working for the development of 'our' young people. It's great to see them now, out and being proud and productive people.

Since the beginning of the Girls' Projects we have been badgered by the media to give them information about 'deprived' and 'problematic' young women. They always wanted access to young women for some book, magazine article or TV programme. Sometimes we complied, but because of my politics and my own experience of being silenced I never wanted to make a 'name' for myself. I have always felt that it was important that young women have the experience of speaking out for themselves: they are the 'stars'. It's been so exciting working with young people. The ideas and opportunities you make available to people when they are young stay with them for the rest of their lives. I was in a privileged position. I was able to put my politics into practice. I was able to build a staff team who were mostly lesbians and we worked very well together. It was the best work situation that I've ever had.

I left because I wanted to try new things and because I felt the project needed new blood. I think I'm a pioneer rather than somebody who can keep things going. My new job at the Haringey Lesbian and Gay Unit is challenging, because once again no one has done it before. This is a chance to make things better for our community. After all we worked for in the Women's Movement and in Gay Liberation, it's off the streets and into the Town Hall! [laughs] I want to break down the silence about us and help us to be recognized for what we are: amazing and important people.

Over the last nine years I have been involved in one of the most important relationships of my life. I met Louie in Bradford when she was a 21-year-old undergraduate; we both called ourselves bisexual then as we were both still involved with men. After our first meeting at a party I went my way and forgot about her. She returned to my life some years later when I saw her performing with a theatre group called the General Will. They put on the first lesbian play at the Bristol Lesbian Conference in 1975. The group were well known on the scene as the 'Bradford Boot Girls'. They were a group of marauding, drunken dykes who wore denims and big Doc Martens (before they became fashionable). I used to watch her at discos when they came to London. I thought she was really attractive, despite the brutal clothes and all the drink she used to get through. After a while Louie came to London to get away from all that and got in contact with me. I was going out with four different women at the time, all at different stages of breaking up and coming together. We got off with each other after a disco and after a while we fell in love. I dropped everyone else. Eventually we moved in together and had this really close, powerful relationship which was based on us looking after each other. I had a very bad back and was often ill and she was always patient and caring, and I can't say how much I appreciated it.

We were living in a grotty 1920s council estate, and though we had made our flat nice it was very tense and we felt a bit paranoid being two lesbians living surrounded by some very unhappy people. In 1981 we decided to buy a house with a friend of ours whom we had extended a lot of love to. The dream turned into a nightmare. She really turned us over, and with her went much of my faith in sisterhood. It ended in a barrister's office in Lincoln's Inn, with one of us at the start of a nervous breakdown.

To get away from the utter depression of the situation Louie went to visit her sister in the States, and while she was away I started a relationship with a woman called Jane. It was meant to be a casual thing as she was involved with someone too, but it soon turned into a compulsion and turned my life upside down. So on the one hand I was having a relationship with Jane that was opening a lot of doors for me, and on the other hand I has having a family life with Louie and our dog Smith. For three years there have been two women in my life and it's been hard on all of us. I never want to experience something like that again. Louie finally left me and we both became ill because of the pain of it all. I'm hoping we'll be able to have some sort of friendship, because she's incredibly important to me. I live with Jane now but the conflicts haven't ceased. I'm trying to live a calm life, trying to find some ease and harmony. When you are a lesbian and politically active there must be some space in your life which is warm and comforting to counteract the hostility of the outside world.

POSTSCRIPT

In the last few months my security has been threatened again. I have had big changes in my personal life which has also meant my home (which is so vitally important to my well being) has been put at risk of being lost. Louie has come to my rescue and we plan to live together again. I am happy about this and hope my stability will be restored. Perhaps the last five years of emotional turmoil will at last be over! I have been sharply reminded once again that my security is very fragile and so crucially dependent on other people's whims. It has seemed like such a struggle just to get a roof over my head: I am forty-five years old and have been working since I was 16; I think I deserve it.

My work is also threatened by Thatcher's government by its attack on lesbian and gay rights and local democracy. Not only has my job been at risk by the cuts in local government spending, but the introduction of Section 28 of the Local Government Act. This Section directly threatens the community that lesbians and gays have struggled so hard to build in the last twenty years. I see this move by the government as a much larger strategy to eliminate all opposition to it, and we can see quite clearly since the mid-seventies the whittling away of rights by legislation, the right-wing media, and police activity to any group who challenges oppression.

One of the most frightening experiences I have had in the last few months has been my visits to the Houses of Parliament to witness the 'debates' around Section 28. The Tories have such a large majority that they do not even have to attempt debate: they just wheel out a lot of drunken upper-class men from the bar at voting time and another pernicious law is born! It was frightening because it was so clear that any opposition has no chance and any expression of tolerance and sense is being swept away. All of us sitting in that House had images of Germany in the 1930s in our minds.

I have been glad to be a part of the struggle against the instatement of this Law and am proud of the way the lesbian and gay communities have fought back. Once again lesbians have been at the

107

forefront of these activities, and the lessons we have learned in the fights against sexism, racism, ableism and other people's rights have come into play.

Last week I was told I had to wear glasses 'for close work'. Yes, middle age is here to stay, but I still feel optimistic (with a little help from my friends) and that can't be bad, can it?

Gilli Salvat, 31 May 1988

HELEN LILLY

INTERVIEWED ON 18 JUNE 1985 BY
MARGOT FARNHAM

My father's family are travelling showmen. They had a tenement
house in Newcastle. I was born in June 1946. My early childhood
was living in my grandmother's showman's wagon. We went on
the Moor and travelled around the Durham Miners' and Bedl-
ington Miners' Gala. One of the first ever things I remember was
the miners' lodge banners; they made a great impression on me.

That was till I was five. And then my dad give it up. He used
to do markets and shows just after the war, in seaside places just
outside of Newcastle. He give it up and he went on the railway.
He thought I should have some type of settled life and wanted to
settle down himself because he'd had a bad time in the army.
He'd come out with industrial dermatitis, and it really made him
bad. They wouldn't give him any compensation, wouldn't pay
him a pension, so he went on the railway and was a member of
the NUR for a long time till he was made redundant. My dad's
family were all active in Labour Party politics, and one of his
uncles was on the Jarrow march which he was quite proud of. My
dad was always active in politics, even though travelling showmen
were quite conservative.

My mother was from down London. She was apprenticed to a
Jewish tailoring firm in Islington. She left school when she was
fourteen and only done it for four years. They said she should
have been a seamstress, but she stuck it out and asked to become
a tailor, so they took her on as an apprentice tailor, which was
quite unusual at that time; quite a step forward for a woman. But
me mother said when she was nineteen she didn't appreciate it.

109

She wanted to go in the army. Her friends were going, all these women she knew all went into the ATS. She could have stayed in it because there was war work and she could have done uniforms, but she said she didn't want to do that; she went into the ATS.

My mother had a very good friend called Eileen and I think it was physical as well. They were both in the big army camps down in Kent. My mother worked on the docks, on the big cargo boats and troop carriers. She said it was quite hairy because it was when bombs were dropping round '41 and '42. Her family are all strong Labour. My grandmother was very strong chapel with Labour connections through primitive Methodism. My mother was much more into having a good time.

My early childhood was very happy actually. Very free. Being a travelling show kid, I had more freedom than other kids, which was nice. When we lived in Newcastle the kids were right urchins, scruffy little cows we were. Nobody had anything; the doors were open. We had two rooms and we were quite well off because me dad was on the NUR. Most of them had very, very little just after the war. It was nice though. We went away for school trips and the neighbours were really nice. We had a community, one of the things I miss now. Everybody used to look after one another's kids. Say that somebody was going out for the day up the park, the mothers used to take all the kids whosever kids they were. And the old weren't neglected by any means. People were looked after. If people went into hospital their homes were cleaned.

We played hopscotch and two balls, top and whip and marbles; different seasons you had different games. It was just after the war, things seemed grey. I remember the ration books. One of the earliest recollections I ever had was of my grandmother when I was about two. She was a drinker all her life and her friend Mrs Bliss, she was a travelling showwoman. My granny was a tall, straight Victorian, and her and Mrs Bliss both used to drink gin like it was going out of fashion. When I was very little, I found the two old girls sitting in the passage with their hats over their eyes. It was really funny because my granny put her hand in her pocket and she gave us half a crown, and said, 'Don't tell your aunt Polly your granny's pissed again.'

The first school I went to was Cambridge Street Infants and Juniors and Seniors. It was one of those all in one Council schools. Everything was in one Victorian building. You started off in the

110

Infants and if you didn't pass your eleven plus you stayed there till you were fifteen. If you did pass, you went to a Grammar School. At eleven you knew you were going into a factory, and you were going to become married. Apart from that I was quite happy at school. From the time I was eleven I used to bunk off. It was just after the war, the fifties; they still had strong discipline and corporal punishment. You got the belt if you were late, this leather strap. I left Cambridge School when our tenement was pulled down. We moved into a flat and I went to a Church of England Secondary School, St Andrew's. But even that was grim. You've seen them: most cities in Britain have got them, this grim, big yard. You've got your play-yard and no beauty.

I became a lesbian when I was fourteen. That's one thing I really am proud of. It's twenty-five years ago last month. I met one of the girls I was at school with, Winnie. We bunked off one afternoon. We never heard the word lesbian, no way, didn't even have any concept of what it was. We had this physical attraction for one another and we went in the park one afternoon and we had an affair. That lasted for about three months. In the park, yes. There was nowhere else. Nobody taught what it was about. It was just one of those things that seemed to come naturally. It was first love, one of those things you never forget. And it happened to be my first love was with a woman. She came from a large working-class family. Her expectations were that she got married, which she did and she's regretted it ever since. She's been divorced twice. She just didn't have the strength enough to fight that through. That's one thing that I'm always grateful for, that my family were possessive enough to not want me to get married. I didn't have that pressure. I had that freedom, which I was really proud of. There was my father's political leaning as well. One of the things he said was, 'You get married if you want to get married. It's a woman's right to choose.'

I remember the only sex education lesson we ever had was in needlework. We had this teacher called Mrs Salsby; I was about thirteen or fourteen. You talked about your periods and where babies come from and that was your sex education. Lesbianism and, God, anything else, well, you had to learn by your mistakes and errors. The rest you got from other girls and what you gleaned from books.

When I was fifteen/sixteen, I was really hooked on a woman

and it was bad. I met her down at a pub in Newcastle. Actually from this time I'd started to think about my sexuality. I realized I was different. I'd had this fling with Winnie and I realized that's what I wanted. I didn't want to trip down the aisle with some fella and have numerous kids.

By this time I was seriously thinking about politics, thinking about joining the Young Socialists. I was fifteen. The Conservatives were in; it was '61, '62. My dad was talking about politics. I was thinking about Newcastle and what was going to happen, because it was pretty bad. Sixty-one was just before I left school; it was when the economic climate was pretty good down the south but was declining in the north. It was starting to bite again. The so-called affluence of the fifties had gone. This was when there was about 200,000 people unemployed in the whole of the country. These were the figures I remember. I think a couple of years later Quentin Hogg came up, wearing his hat and talking about making the north-east, reviving the industries so there would be no more unemployment.

I'd left school and started reading anything political I could get my hands on. A lot of women's books, trade union books, political pamphlets that came out of the Communist party, *The Morning Star*, then I read Marx avidly. I read Engels's *Conditions of the Working Class*. Looking back now there wasn't anybody alive who actively had charisma and influenced me greatly in the early sixties. I'd seen the Stones just before they became popular in '63, '64, because they come to Newcastle. They were really raw. From then on the decline of the sixties began and I started branching out, thinking more for myself. We were all trying to change the world. By then the '64 election was coming up, so we were all knocking on doors, wanting to chuck the Conservatives out. George Brown came up. I went and listened to him and booed him and heckled him. Heckled Labour, heckled the Conservative who was Willy Elliot at the time, because it was Conservative where we lived in western Newcastle. Heath came up.

I think they probably talked more about sexuality in the Young Tories. We talked about women's politics and equal opportunities and how we'd all be equal and stand together on the barricades with guns. That was the whole rhetoric I got carried away with. But it was good and then I joined the CP when I was eighteen. I think it was just a natural progression from the YS into the

Communist Party. I went in because I felt it was the answer. I've got a great affection for the Labour Party but I thought, Oh God, it wasn't going anywhere, and Wilson wasn't making much of an impact. And I found there were a lot of working-class people in when I was in it.

Q: *Can you talk a bit now about the double life you've described yourself as leading?*

What the dives? There was nothing else. The Women's Movement hadn't got off the ground. There was no women-only things. It wasn't that you weren't out as a lesbian, it was just that the pubs were all you had and they were grotty, overcharged and mixed. The pub I frequented was called the Royal Court in Newcastle. It was a dive, where all sorts of people went, you had gays and petty criminals and prostitutes, so you mixed shoulders with everybody. This was the middle sixties. I was into the three-piece suits and the butch thing. I never wore a tie; I couldn't stand them. And no way could I ever see myself as a femme. God, no. It was the high heels [laughs]. You felt you were either one or the other. Country and Western was very fashionable I remember, Patsy Cline, when I was into the Stones meself. Most of the people were in couples. It took you a long time to get in. Also, a lot of the women who were on the game were also lesbian. I lived with a couple of women who were on the game, but I just used to say, 'That's your life; that's separate.'

I slept with one man: it was just that I felt, 'Am I missing something?' After, I knew I wasn't missing anything at all and I knew then what I wanted. I do find my sexuality has always been lesbian. I acted as a butch, but I was never into heavy role-playing. I think when I first got into the bar scene I did it for a little while; then I met a woman who said she couldn't go with a purely butch woman. I felt quite relieved, I'll tell you. Looking back now I couldn't stand that power thing, although I wouldn't have said it in those words then. I became freer in myself, because at one time I felt I was giving out all the time and sometimes you wanted something back as well. Sometimes you wanted to feel close with a woman.

A friend of mine in her seventies, who lives in Newcastle, was telling me once, she'd never let a woman touch her in all her life.

113

She'd been a lesbian for a long, long time and she was saying she'd never let a woman touch her. I thought that was quite sad.

I did say I led a double life, but in the CP I wasn't denying my sexuality at all. Later on, when I was in my twenties, I really found that I was starting to become the token working-class woman. I was in the CP for about five years, from '66 to '71. I left because they were trying to get on the bandwagon and taking up causes but without much thought behind them. I came out of the CP in my early twenties.

When Czechoslovakia came up, I was on my way there, there were six of us going to Prague. And then Paris came up in the May, the students, the revolutionary events. I think we started seeing Prague as the ideal of what we wanted socialism to be, then the tanks came in. And Jan Palach – he was a student who burnt himself to death in Prague in '68 when the Russian troops came in, and that was quite an image in my mind. He was just a working-class man and they'd started saying in the Communist Party that Moscow was right, but if you were a thinking person you knew it was wrong. At the time I thought the Czechs and the Hungarians had a right to determine their own course of socialism. I think everybody has and that's when I started thinking it was wrong. I didn't flee exactly then. A lot of people did leave later on. It's still quite painful actually, because I think if we'd had an independent Communist Party in this country, I might still be in it.

When I was twenty I went in to Newcastle University as a cleaner and I went into NUPE. Before that I had dead-end jobs, I'd been up and down to London. My mother was working as a Senior Cleaner and she said, 'Do you want a permanent job?' I was still in the Communist Party but up and down, living a schizophrenic type of existence during me teens, so I got really involved in NUPE. Though it was a mixed branch, the vast majority of the members were the low-paid domestic cleaners. We had 1,000 members and 800 of them were women. The rest were either porters or boilermen. At one time NUPE got a female membership up to a half a million. It's fallen back now. I was Branch Chairman and Acting Secretary.

I really feel sad about NUPE because they've got potential for women. In my branch at one time the women were all really apathetic. We used to go round and ask women to join: 'I'll have

to ask me dad, I'll have to ask me husband if I join the union.'
But once you got them into the union it was surprising how
radical those women started to become. They started to think,
started to listen. Before I became Chairman if you got ten to go
out of 900 you were lucky. One of the things I did was get an
agreement with the University to have meetings at the workplace,
because a domestic couldn't come from campus down to the main
area. We used to have meetings up in the campus and that's how
we started. It was just really going in and not having any
prejudice and taking the women with you.

We started our own women's group. We started our own paper,
the Newcastle University Women's Broadsheet. Also we had our
own pay agreement as well and we had very good pay and conditions. By this time I was defining myself as a lesbian and getting into
women's politics, but I was finding it very difficult to talk about my
own sexuality. I found their attitudes to their husbands and boyfriends quite revolutionary. Some of the women started talking about
being battered and the brutality of marriage, and the way they were
feeling about their bodies as they were getting older. When we were
talking about sexuality we took in the whole economics of bad housing and economic dependence. We had a couple of widows who
worked who weren't going to get their pensions and one of the resolu-
tions I remember we had was that all women should have the same
pension rights as men. At midday I used to go around and talk,
because that's the only way I found out what was the trouble and
what women wanted, which was better pay and conditions. They also
wanted other things, like a nursery, and we did get maternity leave
and the right to negotiate our own conditions. I took the six points
of the Women's Liberation Movement and we did get them through
the branch, even the demands about the rights of lesbians, and we
managed to pull it through to NUPE conference.

At the '76/'77 conference, when they were starting to talk about
placing five token women on the Committee, I was against that
because the vast majority of the Executive Council were men; the
Area Secretaries were men; the General Secretary was a man.
There was no radical change to bring women in from the bottom.
In NUPE, especially in Scotland and the north-east, we had really
radical women and women who had been in the trade union
movement for a long time who wanted to become Area
Secretaries. We were being fobbed off.

I left because of personal problems, but I am sorry because I left too soon. I think we could have done some really good work, because it was working-class women who were fighting for their own rights. Pay and conditions, people thought that was the only thing they would come out on strike for, but they also came out for the nurses; they were really involved with women's rights. I'd done a couple of TUC courses. NUPE wanted me to go to Ruskin College, but I was really frightened because I can't write very well. It's one of the hang-ups I had from secondary school and one of the things I've always hidden. I actually do feel I did let myself down; I let NUPE down; I let the women down. They all wanted me to take it, but they didn't know the reason why I didn't.

I was also in the women's group at Newcastle University, which was middle class and hard going. I stuck it for a few months. They were talking abut heterosexuality and because I was out as a lesbian, and a working-class lesbian, I felt a token like I did in the CP. I think that's been the crux of the matter, this split between heterosexuals and lesbians. Lesbians felt they put their heart and soul in. They've supported heterosexual women in the past but whenever we've asked for help, suddenly they've scurried away and you never see no one. We've always been stood there on our own ultimately. That's why later on I became a separatist.

I lived in Radnor Terrace. I went squatting for a bit and lived in women-only houses. That's all to do with the fact that ultimately that's how I would like to live. When I became a separatist I thought of the women from my work at Newcastle and I wished I could have brought them with us, because when I lost contact I felt I lost something. I admired their life: how they'd brought up their kids, how they'd taken adversity and laughed at it. I'm not looking through rose-coloured glasses and I'm not looking back in hindsight: I find them really strong. I mean they're strong and they're weak but I feel the Women's Movement has never been able to get close enough to those women.

Q: *You were saying that when you were thirty you got involved in a lesbian marriage?*

I met this woman, Jackie, and we had an affair, but I think we wanted society to accept us, to know that two women could make it. At the time we both needed security. She was into the whole

116

matriarchal magic bit. I've got to admit that I can't stand that, but anyway I loved the woman at the time, so when she suggested that we got married and have a Romany wedding, we did. We had a fire and jumped the brush, exchanged gold wedding rings, cut one of our wrists. Quite painful. I've still got the scar actually. We thought it was going to last. We were together nearly three years but after about two months of this we both felt trapped. Looking back it was this whole thing of being trapped into monogamy and houses and getting a job, working and looking after somebody for the next forty years. It was really screwing us up. God knows how heterosexual women stick it. It's taken me and Jackie till last year really to become friends again, and I did love the woman and still care for her very much.

I've lived with five women over all, a year and longer. I've lived with a woman for the past six years and it was very monogamous in the beginning. We had a really good relationship and when the physical side finished, instead of just parting, we both stayed friends and we worked our relationship into an emotional thing, and that was really nice. Though she's moved out now, we had a very strong relationship.

The person I am now to the person I was, say, six or seven years ago is totally different. I've calmed down a lot. I have to admit now that I left active politics because I was drinking, couldn't cope. The woman, Di, I was living with helped stop me drinking and I had therapy as well. Therapy can help you up to a point but ultimately you've got to help yourself. I was in the trade union movement where drinking was accepted, everybody drank. In my family, drinking is accepted. Me dad was a very heavy drinker. Whatever I did there was drink, the labour movement, the bar scene and that's a bad thing I think.

Q: *How do you socialize now?*

I go to the older lesbian group. I still go into bars and discos but I don't drink half as much as I did. I went to the Older Lesbian Network because I wasn't active in politics for a long time. I wanted to discuss ageism and certain things like this. But they didn't talk about these things to the extent I wanted. Now it's just really social. I've met some really lovely women through it and women who years ago I would never have met. Women like myself who've been in politics, women who've gone through the bar scene, women who are quite closeted. I'd like to get into more active working-class politics, not just lesbian politics.

Q: *How close are you to your family now?*

I'm still very close to my mother. My dad died the year before last. I still see my family on numerous occasions and I still get invited to the weddings and funerals. They know that I'm a lesbian. They don't care. In fact they still call me by my old name, which is Lilian. I changed my name to Helen, because I couldn't stand Lilian, and at various stages I used to be known as Geordie as well in the bar scene. That has very heavy connotations and that's one of the reasons I changed my name to Helen. When I changed my name, I gave up the butch image. I think names can make you feel different and Helen did make me feel a lot different. If you had met me say six years ago, I'd have been really aggressive. Now I do feel a lot freer, more relaxed, a better person, actually, than I was fifteen years ago. And it's nothing to do with age.

LAURA JACKSON

INTERVIEWED ON 16 JANUARY 1988 BY
JAYNE EGERTON

I was born in Southampton in 1954 and had a working-class background. My mother was working in a factory at the time and my father was a student. My mother's parents had been very involved in working-class movements. My grandmother worked in school kitchens and my grandfather at a smelting works. They'd been through the thirties together, had strong feelings about poverty and fought hard for the welfare state. Both of them were in the Communist Party when I was younger.

My mother was a trade union activist but my father wasn't interested in politics at all. My father's background was a farming community in Wales. Until I was seven we lived in a traditional, close-knit working-class community. They were all council houses with passageways leading into each other's back gardens. It was very friendly: everyone helped each other. We all played out in the streets as kids. It always seemed to be the women who were dominant in that community. Generally you stayed in the community because your mother lived there.

I've got a younger sister who was born when I was eleven. My aunt had twin sons and I played with them. I was a very sociable child. There was always a gang. At that stage it was mixed and I wasn't very conscious of the differences between boys and girls. I didn't really start to be aware of the fact that I was more friendly with girls until I was in the Junior school. I was generally regarded as a very pretty child with classical blond hair and blue eyes, and I was made a lot of fuss of.

My mother wanted a boy very badly and was very distraught

119

In dress studio, 1957

when I was born, and they carried on calling me Phillip – which was the name they were going to give to a boy – until I was about two. My mum was very reluctant to give my gender away when I was a baby to people who looked at me in the pram. But then she got into it, I think, because I emerged as being pretty in her eyes. She always bought me beautiful clothes and dressed me up. I was like a little doll really. At about three or four she used to put rollers in my hair every night. I must have looked ridiculous actually, because I was always the frilly, pretty little girl in this gang.

My relationship with my mother wasn't good. She was very domineering and I got hit a lot by her. Now I can understand why. I think it's because my father always gave preference to me in many ways over her. When they could afford a car it was always me that got taken out for a ride. She was the one who went out to work, and when she wasn't working she was doing the housework. She wasn't around a great deal and she always seemed preoccupied.

I was about four when my father started abusing me. It's hard to remember the actual detail. It's patchy. I did what a lot of survivors do, which is to block out a lot. It's like a lot of missing jigsaw pieces which I've gradually been trying to put together for the last five years. There are days when I get a sudden realization about something else that happened.

When my mother was working and he was looking after me at home he wanted to teach me to read. I used to sit on his lap and he'd read to me. Then he started giving me pornography to look at and asking me what was in the pictures, and I'd tell him. He'd say it was dirty and rude. I knew that meant something wrong, so in the end I stopped telling him what was in the pictures. I'd make it up and he'd say I was lying. Then he'd look at me in a very piercing way and say he was a wizard and knew what was in my mind. That's the bit that used to frighten me. Sometimes he'd take me upstairs and that's where I get blocks. I remember kneeling over a bed but not much more, and I do remember waking up at night with a dreadful smell and my eyelids being held down. I don't know why or when I had this sense of waking up and not being able to physically open my eyes. I do know that it was awful and that I felt totally powerless. I wet the bed until I was about eleven, probably because of all this. I always seemed to have itching and a rash between my legs and dreadful pains in my lower abdomen. I was sick a lot as well. I was always in pain when I was a child.

What's affected me most is the total abuse of trust. I'm still left with this dreadful fear of him in my head. The fear of him being psychic and knowing what I'm thinking. I must have been affected by the physical abuse but that isn't what upsets or makes me angry now, it's the emotional side and what he succeeded in doing to me and my mother. I think it stopped when I went to school.

But even when I was older he treated me as his best friend and confidante. I was very close to him. Apart from the abuse he did look after me a lot. I admired him because he was clever and I always knew he'd help me with my school-work. I loved and respected him. I felt as if I was almost his equal. It changed when I was an adolescent, because I started thinking about men in general and power, and reading feminist books. I also became very aware that he was treating my mother very badly. He belittled her a lot. My mother finds it difficult to read and write, and he used to use that and tell her she was stupid. When she got very fat he used to laugh at her. He influenced me completely about my mother and made me believe she was stupid, illiterate and ugly. So I was never going to be fat, I wanted to be as clever as possible and I was never going to be as clingy as she had been.

Now I feel really angry with him: the power he had to make her feel that way about herself and to make me feel that way about her too. We're only just beginning to establish a relationship, my mother and I, so in a way he won completely. I feel like I'm more aware of the issues than my mother and I've got a lot of support from women I can talk to. But my mother has nobody really, she's really left with it: a broken marriage and thirty-three years of not knowing why her and I didn't get on, and feeling that she's failed. My father's schizophrenic now. I was about fifteen at the time when he left. He started having affairs. He got into drugs and crime and began losing control of his life. When the divorce came through he didn't pay maintenance for my sister and me and didn't send any birthday cards. He cut himself off completely.

When I was eleven I went to a mixed-sex, purpose-built comprehensive school. My primary school had been tyrannical. So I loved it. It was progressive and encouraged young people to think. We had lots of discussions on controversial subjects, and working in groups. It was the heyday of the sixties and there was a future. Lots of the teachers had been to Oxford or Cambridge but were left-wing and believed politically in comprehensive education. The school was very democratically run. We had our own pupil council right from the first year. I was in the Revolutionary Young Socialists, a junior branch of what was then the International Socialists, which later became the Socialist Workers Party. I was very much into class struggle and the revolution. A few of us had also become involved in the School Kids Union. We did loads of things. We used to be thrown out of school during break in the winter and we didn't like it. We called everybody into the playground, stormed the building and refused to move. It was amazing to think that these little First Years agreed to it as well! [laughs] We won that one.

After that we decided to take it on a grand scale. We started leafleting about school students' rights outside schools. We'd call meetings and campaign around issues like contraception in loos, getting boys who were thrown out because of the length of their hair reinstated and Schoolkids' Unions. All the meetings were crowded. We eventually affiliated to the local Trades Council and when it came to the May Day Rally we led the march. There were school uniforms hoisted on poles and burnt and *Little Red School Books* sold and given out to kids in the street. The police tried to confiscate them!

My first big demonstration as a school student was in London with the NUS. The campaign was all about how Thatcher, who was Education Minister, wanted to control school funds. It was the miners' strike at the same time. When we were in Trafalgar Square someone said that the miners were coming down the road, so we joined in with them and tried to storm the National Coal Board. It was so exciting. We all thought that this was what we were here for. Everything we'd worked for, we'd read about, we'd talked about in our groups: we were here now with the miners, fifth row from the front.

I remember a woman from Women's Liberation coming to speak to us about the 'demands' as they were then. She talked a lot about equal pay and abortion. My peer group was really impressed. I think it really spoke to us. We'd also started reading things like *The Female Eunuch*. We were very clear about saying to the boys that they'd got to know their place and they couldn't take control. I also remember a lot of equal pay strikes at the time. My mum was on strike a lot. There was a lot of militancy, and I don't think it was just because I was involved in left-wing groups and knew about it.

It was a bloody shambles at home at this time. There were fights and rows, and there were also screaming matches between my father and I for the first time. It was me who told him to get out in the end. I confided in my friends. We used to talk about everything. We decided we were going to have a consciousness-raising group in the sixth form block in the coffee bar. We used to do weird things, like touch each other in a sexual way and then talk about our feelings. We wanted to experience everything, we wanted to explore everything, we wanted to understand everything. We wanted to know who Jean Paul Sartre was!

Before the sixth form my two best friends and I lost our virginity at the same time. There was a lot of pressure on us to sleep with boys, and also we were very much a product of the sixties. We all went to the same party and there were lots of older boys there. We all decided we were going to do it together that night. We all dragged boys upstairs to separate bedrooms and emerged very sheepishly. It was a functional thing for all of us. We all thought it was boring, without exception. At that time we thought it was because the boys we slept with were boring, but later on we came to terms with the fact that it was boring full stop.

I was quite demonstrative and physical with girls until I was about fifteen but then it stopped. Even when I was at Junior school I remember clearly my best-friend and I playing photographers and touching each other and being beside myself with excitement, and at secondary school I had another best-friend and we used to play together. It was her who said to me, when we were about fourteen, that we should stop doing this now and start going out with boys. I became very wholehearted about going out with boys. I definitely fancied boys. I fancied girls as well but it wasn't really in my frame of reference to even think about doing anything about it. I'd heard the term lesbian in a derogatory way, but I didn't know any. The stereotype I had in my head told me I didn't look like one, so I couldn't be one.

We all went out with boys but our real love was with each other. We saw each other every day and talked all the time about what we did and how we felt. We laughed a lot about the boys.

We thought that men's willies were ridiculous. I began feeling unsatisfied. Sex was really boring. I read the right articles in the right magazines and knew that men wanted you to have orgasms, so I faked them all the time. My expectation of boys wasn't very high, and my emotional life was with my best-friends.

By this time I was in the sixth form and a bit more open to thinking about other possibilities. I was very lucky because I was in an environment where gay politics was at least on the agenda. I started to have so many sexual dreams about women and I always woke up far more sexually aroused than by anything else. I found I was into women through these dreams. So I talked to John, who was a gay boy in the sixth form and he was very calm and said I needed to come to this club with him that night, and that's how I got on the gay scene. It was called the Moulin Rouge, and we called it the Moulie.

The first time I walked in I was hit by how plush it was: red carpet, chandeliers, a cocktail bar and a long bar. I was amazed. I'd not been to a night-club before. I had on loons, a cotton T-shirt with bell sleeves, my platform shoes and a velvet jacket, and I had very long hair and the usual eye make-up. I was shocked by the butch lesbians and didn't fit in at all really. Several of the women came up and first of all talked to John and asked questions about me and one of them asked me to dance. I was dead nervous. They asked if I was queer or bisexual, and because I hadn't had a sexual relationship with a woman as an adult I said bisexual. So they were quite hostile to me. I didn't like the word queer and I was very surprised to hear gays and lesbians using the term: I thought they wouldn't want to. I started using it too, of course, when I got into the gay scene.

There was a big class divide in the club itself between men and women. The women were predominantly working class and most of the men were middle class. The women were mainly older than me and there was a shortage of femmes. Most of the femmes were not available because if you were a femme you were hooked up pretty quick. There were quite a few women who worked in the same factory as my mum, two who worked on building sites (one of whom passed for a man). There were a lot of 'screws', and an ex-policewoman, and the rest did things like low-level sales work.

It was a really schizophrenic existence, because during the day I would be very vocal at school, talking about politics and campaigning, then I'd go home and get changed out of my jeans and into my little black evening dress, and go up to the club where I'd start to behave in a very feminine way. I feel that being a femme was imposed on me by that particular subculture, because of the way I looked. If you had long hair you were a femme, it didn't matter what you wore. Sometimes, in fact, I liked wearing contradictory clothes, so I'd wear lots of eye make-up and curl my long blond hair, but wear a suit with a tie. The first night I watched the way that women with long hair didn't get up and ask anyone to dance. Later on when I started going every night I'd ask women to dance and I really got told off. One femme gave me hell and said she wasn't going to dance with me if she was paid! So I learnt the rules in that way. I could have cut my hair but I liked it, and it was also part of the youth subculture that I was involved in outside of the club, which was to do with Left teenage politics.

I was quite a bolshie femme on the scene once I'd had my own lover, Pat, who protected me. I didn't ever tolerate the behaviour that some of the femmes tolerated from their butch lovers: the violence, and the way they'd talk about the femmes in front of them. It was fairly stereotypical language about being a wife. Bearing in mind that I'd seen my mother being humiliated by my father I was not going to put up with that. There were women who changed their names to male names and tried to live as men. They didn't want to see themselves as women. I felt they were into doing something sexually to women but weren't going to lower themselves to be in that position. Butches had a really good grasp of humiliation and degradation. They knew something which a lot of femmes didn't know really, which is that men hate and are disgusted by women. They were not going to make themselves vulnerable as women who are passive do. I think now it's about self-loathing, woman hating and being disgusted with your own body. It saddens me because I think men have made us hate our bodies so much.

There was an unwritten rule that 'stone' butches were never touched, the femmes would be touched. The first two women I went out with on the straight gay scene didn't want to sleep with me. I didn't ever find out why with one of them, but it was awful with the other one. She kept all her clothes on. I couldn't believe it. In the end she started crying and said she'd been raped by her brother and his friends when she was younger and couldn't ever

Margate, 1960

have anyone touch her. I think there are a lot of 'stone' butches who have been abused in the past: however, I think there are a lot of femmes who have been too. Many of us have been very 'loose' in the way we've allowed ourselves to be touched. So I don't think abuse means only that you can't be touched. It can mean both and it's not clear why you go one way and not the other.

I was very lucky because the butch woman who I did have a fairly long relationship with was a classic case of butch on the streets and femme in the sheets. I was delighted! It was my fantasy come true. She was very much into being passive but suffered a lot in terms of her self-esteem. I was never to tell anybody and when we were telling crude jokes about what you were doing in bed she'd always align herself with the butches. I didn't ever give her away. There may have been more flexibility in roles behind the scenes. I wish I'd known then as it would have made our conversations much more interesting than being about this ridiculous role-play. It was like going into some other time, it was very old fashioned, very masculine and feminine. It was about being dainty or chivalrous. Those kind of words come up. Yet outside it was a time of political awareness, unisex, and the beginnings of women's liberation. They didn't ever touch that scene at all. We hardly ever referred to them.

The classic scenario on a Saturday night was that we'd dress up and walk into the club together. I'd usually be in a dress or long skirt and Pat would be immaculately dressed in her three piece suit, tie, brylcreem and winklepickers. The femmes would usually be dropped with the other femmes at one of the little tables and the butches would carry on walking down to the far end of the bar and they'd order her a feminine drink, usually a short. I got very bored with that and insisted on going down to the bar with Pat. I don't think a lot of butches liked that, but Pat was really good. She was attracted to me in a way because I was a bit wild and didn't go along entirely with the rules.

Pat was a lovely woman, very generous and warm. She looked after me completely. She was in her thirties when I was seventeen and had a very different history. Her whole life had been about being on the gay scene. I was a reckless youngster in terms of emotions and wanted to go to University and travel. I wasn't going to stay in the rut I'd been brought up in. She thought it was quite sweet that she had this young lover who used to go on demonstrations, but she wasn't interested in any of that.

Our sexual relationship was very exciting. It was quite sado–masochistic in terms of fantasy, and very heavy penetration and dressing-up. But it was never violent. She didn't ever hit me. There was a lot of telling each other fantasies. I was addicted to it and found it really difficult to sleep with anyone else. I did love her but we didn't have anything in common after a while, apart from sex. I didn't want this role play anymore. I didn't want anyone else to be masochistic with me. It made me feel really bad about myself. I also wanted to feel happier about being passive. I was passive sometimes but it didn't really do anything for me. It was still like being with the boys. I wasn't really excited by it and I wanted to be one day.

I have to say that despite violence in a lot of relationships, there was a great deal of love and caring in that community. Women would do anything for each other. If anyone was in trouble, if anyone was going to get the sack for being 'queer', they would all support each other. They'd share money, they'd share their flats. But it didn't ever occur to me that my feminist politics might have anything to do with my sexuality. I only thought there was this seedy club scene. I was only just beginning to be able to see a connection between women being lesbians and women's liberation. This was by no stretch of the imagination what women's liberation was saying at the time. I was reading all these dreadful things about men and it seemed to make sense not having relationships with them. Yet I couldn't quite make the connection given that the relationships that seemed to be going on between women were so outrageously stupid and outdated.

I left the country to escape a whole combination of things. My parents' separations had exhausted me and I did want to get away from my relationship with Pat. So I went to Finland for a year as an *au pair*. I loved it. I could just start afresh.

I came back the following summer as I'd applied for a place at Liverpool University because my best friend Anne was supposed to be going there. Towards the end of my relationship with Pat I'd started to have a sexual relationship with her. It was equal, with no kind of role-play. Pat was very upset as she had no frame of reference to understand women who looked like each other having relationships. But when I came back from Finland Anne had decided to live with a bloke. I was shocked. It was very hard for us to speak. She said she couldn't bear to be a lesbian. That was the end of the road for me. My reason for not wanting to be a lesbian was because of the role-play and yet when I found an equal relationship this woman said she wanted to be a heterosexual. I felt there was absolutely no reason to be a lesbian. I assumed I'd be unhappy. I suspected it was the only thing that would ever excite me sexually but I thought my sanity was probably more important than my sexual desire.

I went to Liverpool and started going to the Women's Centre, but I still didn't want to be a lesbian. I was involved in setting up a street theatre group and we used to perform in the centre of Liverpool and pull a crowd. The issues we focused on were unpaid work in the home and Benyon's anti-abortion bill (and later Corrie's). I moved into the Women's Centre around this time, which was a terrible mistake. You lived your politics and the phone was always ringing. There were always women who'd been beaten up arriving. It was like a refuge.

I then started having a relationship with a woman. It was disappointing. I didn't want a relationship with her really but she did introduce me to radical feminism. She was a great theorist. I was really critical of Left politics and men on the Left by this time. I got thrown out of IS by these very heavy boys just before I left home, for failing to go to three meetings and for going to a women's meeting. Since I'd been in Liverpool I'd seen the male Left in action and I was really disgusted. They were very misogynist.

I was missing Pat desperately. There was a National Lesbian Conference and I'd come down with a load of women from Liverpool. It was really bizarre because in the evening there was a social at the Moulin Rouge. I wouldn't talk about my past then. I was really ashamed of it. I knew some of the women who worked behind the bar and they were all taking the piss out of these feminists who were taking their tops off when they were dancing! Here I was with all these wonderful lesbians and I was aching for Pat. I phoned her up and she came over and we slept together that night but I was still not happy. I didn't want to be a lesbian if I was only getting turned on by a lover who I'd done all those things with.

Occasionally when I went to Southampton I'd seen this older

130

brother of some friends of mine called Andy. We'd always got on well and were good drinking pals. He phoned me up one day and said he felt like getting away, so he came up for the weekend. It's very interesting that it was just when I was about to get into radical feminism. We were together for five years. I was twenty-one when it began and still at University. I was blissfully happy for two years. There were no roles. He was very feminine, gentle and open. It was really peaceful. There was no more struggling. I was ostracized from the women's community, but it seemed a small price to pay, given that I thought I'd found heaven.

Then after two years I got pregnant and had a menstrual extraction. After that I stopped sleeping with him for a long time. I'd got back into women's things again and I wanted to break out. I wanted to leave him because I'd changed again. I was really involved in the Reclaim the Night marches and the Women's Newsletter. The composition of women's groups had changed now and most of the women were lesbians. I loved being with women and was beginning to feel really bad about the contradiction of living with him, even though he was really nice. I pushed him a lot at this point, in terms of asking him if he'd been affected by pornography. At first he'd deny it and I'd say he was lying and all men were affected by it. Once he broke down in tears and said it was true and of course he was going to see women like that. Then I'd say I bet he saw me like that. I really pushed him to make him tell me what was going on in his head and I started to realize that this perfect relationship just couldn't be perfect. If he couldn't experience the world in the same way as me what hope was there for genuine equality? So I started removing myself from him a bit. I didn't sleep with anybody else at all, but he slept with lots of my women friends. I used to watch him at mixed parties and he knew he could probably get into bed with any of the feminists because he'd done all the right reading and he'd learned a lot from me. I was getting really angry.

When I got offered my first teaching job, in London, I decided to break away from him as well. I didn't know anybody, I hated my job and I was really lonely, but at the same time I was going to give it a good try. I started going to women-only things on Saturdays at places like Camden Town Hall. I didn't know anyone but I used to go and get pissed and come home. I felt great because I'd not seen so many lesbians in one place. Then one night an old friend of mine from Liverpool introduced me to a woman who was a visiting lecturer over from Australia. I was doing a part time MA in education with reference to Women's Studies, and she was interested in a talk one of my tutors was giving. As soon as she walked in the door I fell head over heels in love with her. We both knew. We walked out of the talk, went to the pub and carried on talking all night. We didn't ever go to bed together. It was funny but she was the catalyst that helped me make the final leap. I knew that it was possible to feel very sexually attracted to somebody and yet feel okay emotionally and intellectually as well.

So here I was at last on my own, a lesbian feminist with a very clear view that I did want to be a lesbian now and that there were political reasons as well as my sexuality. What's more I might be able to find some of the feminists attractive! So the first thing I did was I went to a lesbian group at Haringey Women's Centre and made lots of friends there. Then I had a relationship with one of the women there. It was sleeping with her that changed everything for me because I was really into it. It was really nice and exciting, but gentle. Then at about that time I went to a Women's Research and Resources Centre talk on sexuality and male violence, and that changed my political position again. I heard women like Pat Mahoney, Margaret Jackson and Sheila Jeffreys talking about their own research. I was blown away. I thought it was a brilliant analysis and that this was what I wanted to be involved in.

I joined Central London Women Against Violence Against Women. I poured my energy into talks, campaigns and pickets. My whole life was about campaigning against male violence. We were such an impassioned group. I think we worked very hard at drawing public awareness to what men do to women. I was still doing a part time MA and I decided to focus a lot of my study time on male violence. It was a good combination, campaigning but at the same time having the opportunity to study and read. There seemed to be a hell of a lot going on at that time where it was becoming very public that men abuse, violate and murder women (i.e., the Sutcliffe killings). I poured a lot of my past history and anger into this work. The slogan used to be 'Women are angry' but anger got lost somewhere along the line and what I started to feel was afraid. I had a hell of a lot of fear that was picked up from my past life. I'd just started to realize the scale of men's hatred, and I thought my life would never be the same again and that women's lives were under a state of siege. I've not really been somebody who likes to go into self-analysis and I didn't ever explore that fear until I left WAVAW and got involved with a woman who really helped me look at my fear.

Most of my relationships before Mary were fairly superficial. I found it very difficult to receive and be vulnerable in any way. Only with Mary did it all change. She worked for a women's counselling organization. I had years and years worth of work to do on myself with her. It was well overdue. We were both still doing practical stuff like setting up the Hackney Girls' Refuge, but trying to work things out in our own heads too; it was good. I got involved in the Child Sexual Abuse Preventative Education Project, which was an offshoot of the Incest Survivors Group and was women youth workers and teachers who were counselling and supporting girls who had been sexually abused. I did some campaigning work, training and talks, and then it folded. It was a great shame. Now there's no longer the networks to support the work that we're all doing.

Most of my work now is in schools, partly because I don't know where the Women's Movement is anymore and partly because that's where I spend most of my time. I come into contact with young women every day and I hear what's happening to them and this is where I can have some input. I'm in a more powerful position now as the head of a Humanities department in a girls' school, so I can use that to set things up. I've been writing a unit and making materials for kids to use on male violence, supplemented by resistance work by feminists. It's the first year that I've done it in a structured way and set it as an extra exam piece, and it's been brilliant. The girls have really responded to it. It's the thing that's really gripped them because they all have experience of it in some way and feel very angry about it. It's meant that some of them who are being abused have come to talk to me.

I'm going to a course run by the Child Sexual Abuse Unit at North London Poly at the moment. There's a lot of women from diverse professional groups there who all feel quite isolated and frustrated and want to set something up, so that is exciting. Again that's the work of feminists. It's *not* been something which has

133

come from within the institution, which is the way the institution and the state likes to tell it. It's because of our blood and our sweat that they've got the unit. There's so much being discussed now that we put on the map, but feminists have been made invisible. The state is attempting to take hold of an issue which it has an inaccurate analysis of. There are a lot of telephone lines being set up for kids presupposing that 'disclosure' is enough without necessarily changing the family unit.

I'm hoping that out of the course we might be able to train women teachers in counselling techniques for survivors, and also do public feminist education through schools to balance up some of this dreadful rubbish that's going into schools at the moment from the state.

Changes in government legislation like the Education Act and Clause 28 are terrifying. It's not only going to affect my entire life but all the work that lots of us have been doing for years. I worry that anything that's remotely questioning will be outside the 'core curriculum' which the government wants in schools. I went into education because I wanted to encourage kids to think and question. I can't see the point of my work otherwise.

Thinking about my life as a lesbian now I feel I've changed so much. I have a lot more understanding of what sisterhood and loving women means than I ever have before. I find it much easier to be loved. I don't think I would have felt that if I hadn't started loving myself. A few years ago I would have laughed at that idea. I'm very, very happy. I love being a lesbian. If I had to say what I wanted for lesbians in the future it would be about learning from each other and being prepared to change. I see us supporting each other more, and I don't just mean emotionally. I want the Women's Movement to be resurrected. We still need our freedom so badly and I know we will come back.

MEGAN THOMAS

INTERVIEWED ON 22 OCTOBER 1986 BY
JAYNE EGERTON

I was born in South Wales in 1955. We were there for six months and then we moved to Notting Hill Gate because my father transferred from the Glamorgan to the Metropolitan Police Force. He had a very uniformed past: from school to army to cop shop. Looking back, I think I didn't fit in well with my parents' plans. They'd got their two kids, the son and the daughter, and dad was planning on a change of career and moving up to London. I came along at a very inconvenient time. My mum does refer to me as the hole in the contraceptive.

I had a comfortable childhood in the material sense. I never had to worry about getting food or clothing or a warm bed. But there was very little physical contact in my family. I can only remember once when my dad cuddled me and sat me on his lap and I can never remember my mother cuddling me. In fact, when my mother got pissed off with me she often used to shut me in the cupboard where dad kept his uniforms. That's one of the reasons why I don't go on marches where there are a lot of coppers, because if I get surrounded by uniforms which have got that certain smell I freak out a bit.

As a child I did feel closer to my mother because I saw more of her, but looking back I think that if I'd been given the opportunity I would have been closer to my father – which really throws Freud, because I should be out there looking for a father substitute now. So how I turned out to be a dyke doesn't fit his philosophy.

It was obvious from an early age that I wasn't going to be satisfied with wearing frocks and pushing dolls around, I wanted

135

Lambeth, London, 1985. Portrait by Nicky West

to be out climbing and building go-carts. So I found myself playing more with boys than girls. I think it really helped that my sister was ultra feminine so my parents had someone to work all that stuff out on.

In the first primary school I went to, a mixed Anglican Church school, the girls played up on the playground on the roof and the boys played downstairs, and I was always sneaking downstairs with a couple of other girls, simply because I felt the games the boys were playing were more active, like wrestling, football, cowboys and Indians, and gangsters and robbers. I couldn't abide a lot of girls, I had the same attitude to them as the boys had: 'bloody sissies'. Then I went to an ordinary secular primary school and my close friends were two girls who were similar to me. We were quite renowned in that school. We didn't get slagged off by the boys at all, in fact the more stereotyped girls would get picked on. They had quite a bit of respect for us because they knew that if they treated us like they treated the other girls, they wouldn't get us in floods of tears, they'd get a smack in the face.

My secondary modern school was an all girls' school, and it was horrible. I had no outlet for what I'd previously accepted as the norm. Its educational emphasis was on getting girls into certain types of jobs, because they were only going to be there for a short time before leaving to get married. I'd failed the eleven plus which was no surprise as I was really known as the class clown. Secondary school is where the rot really set in. Instead of being in a situation where I could grow I felt I was always being told off, called out, made to stand outside the classroom. It was almost a constant battle to be yourself. Myself and a couple of other girls with similar backgrounds were very much poked fun at. When other girls were getting boyfriends I just didn't have any interest in boys as sexual partners. I wanted to be with boys because I wanted to be allowed to do the things that they did. I suppose over a period of time I became worn down, despondent and withdrawn at school. I lost a lot of my clowning abilities and became almost a non-entity. I felt that I was being forced to grow up and leave my childhood behind. At twelve I was told that it was about time I stopped playing football and playing with go-carts, and yet it was quite acceptable for boys to continue playing. I did resent that. The girls were preoccupied with the size of their tits and who fancied them, and I found it so restricting.

I felt I had to take an interest in boys because everybody else was doing it. At that time, although I wasn't interested in anything remotely sexual, I was looking for something, some kind of expression. I was about fourteen when I first went along to an Evangelical meeting. There was a disco beforehand and then we went into this youth centre where there were actually girls playing snooker. I thought this was great and felt really comfortable. After a chat and tea we went into a tent where an Evangelist was going on about finding yourself in God. It seemed to give me a lot of answers, and I got totally into it. I was attracted to it because it gave me a way of expressing a lot of feelings that were being subdued at secondary school. I felt that I fitted in and was accepted. It was the Jesus Movement. I could go to these meetings in my jeans and T-shirts and cropped hair and nobody would say anything, and it was okay for me to organize a game of football. There wasn't a lot of dogma attached to it; there wasn't the emphasis on one sexual partner and marriage. It seemed to be a movement geared to adolescent feelings.

I started going out with boys at this time, but there's not much attraction to be found in a spotty-faced 15-year-old boy. I remember I had a life-sized David Cassidy poster on my wall and dad came in and said he looked more like a bloody girl than a bloke, so whether that was the underlying attraction I don't know, but I can never remember looking at a bloke and thinking I really fancied him around that time. If only I'd known there was an alternative, if only somebody had told me about lesbianism, or it was advertised in the early seventies as it is in the eighties. I knew homosexuals existed but I didn't know what the hell they were: spinsters who wore tweed skirts and brogues, and blokes with lipstick and dresses on. But looking back I did feel more drawn to girls.

I remember my first impression of boys was wondering what all the fuss was about. I was really disappointed because sex had been built up and was supposed to be a wonderful experience, but I would have preferred to be playing football or pool with them. I began to think it was me, so I screwed around a little bit more thinking it was just a question of finding the right bloke. But the actual look of a naked fella that I was supposed to feel attracted to just made me think, 'My god, isn't he ugly? Poor bastard, imagine walking around like that?' Even then I didn't realize I might have feelings for other girls.

I suppose because of my disappointment with sex and not having any close relationships, I began to get more into religion, and at about fifteen to feel the Jesus Movement wasn't satisfying me. I felt drawn to more ritualized religion and found myself reading about Catholicism, and then I stepped into a Catholic church and as soon as I saw the statues and candles and smelled the incense, that was it. I started reading about the mystics and got totally swept up into it. Then I read about nuns, and nuns are women, and I felt very drawn to being a nun because I could be with other women. I wasn't aware of any sexual feelings. At that stage I would probably have argued that nuns weren't lesbians, they wanted to be brides of Christ. Over the next year I went to classes in catechism, visited convents, got confirmed and went to workshops at convents and retreats. Then I met a priest from Ireland and he gave me an introduction to the Sisters of Mercy. I went over to stay with them for a few weeks and then the Mistress of Postulants wrote to me and said that they were willing to accept me as a postulant, so I packed my bags and went. My parents had resigned themselves from when I was very young to the fact I was always going to do something different.

When I arrived it was amazing. They met me off the boat in Dublin and we drove to the convent. As soon as I walked into the refectory there were about forty nuns, and each of them in turn came up and gave me a great big hug. It was a wonderful experience. I was a postulant for nine months and did some basic religious studying, but spent most of it getting involved with the work that they do, like helping out in the hospital. Then at the end of the nine months I took the veil as a novice for two years.

You study church history, theology, aspects of the religious life, and that's all you do. You rarely go out of the convent where the noviciate is based. It was two years of rigorous study, prayer, and a daily chore in either the kitchen or laundry. I took a diploma in theology at the end; I would have been a stuffy old theologian if I'd stayed. There were fifteen other novices and I felt very much a part of a family. When I finished my noviciate I went to help out at a primary school at one of our houses. I was only meant to be there for six weeks but I stayed for nearly seven months because I met and got totally besotted by a nun called Sister Mary Gerrity. I couldn't say it was sexual attraction, but just to be in her company was really wonderful. We used to spend hours together talking. I would be in her room till four o'clock in the morning and as a result I sometimes missed morning prayer and even mass. I began to get into trouble. I had all these feelings in me. I was supposed to be dedicating my life to the love of God and I kept thinking about Mary. I got so confused. Also at that time there was an intellectual battle going on inside me. The Roman Church has strict views about what is what, and you don't accept it because your reason tells you, you accept it because faith tells you. So whenever you come across a problem where you can't accept something through your intellect, they immediately say it's a crisis of faith. Emotionally you can feel very drawn to it but intellectually you know it can't be true; like, for example, the Virgin Birth.

Surprisingly enough I also had arguments with a lot of their attitudes to women, although I wasn't aware of my feminism at that time. The Church either saw women as battery hens or saints, you could either be a bride of man or a bride of God. At that point it was difficult because the actual community life was really nice. But I couldn't accept a lot of the dogma when I began going out and seeing exactly what it was doing to other women: women were forced to live in situations where they had about eight kids and were consumed by looking after them, with no support from husbands who were usually very drunk and violent. I just thought that it could not be right and that God had not meant this. I felt the Catholic Church was following the teachings of Paul of Tarsus not Jesus of Nazareth. That got me into a lot of trouble. I wrote an essay on it, which Sister Kathleen tore up in my face. I think if it had been a couple of hundred years ago I would have been burned as a heretic. It was easy to leave from the intellectual point of view but hard emotionally, because that was my family and I was very close to some of the novices. I had a progression of arguments, so I think that if I hadn't left myself I probably would have been told to leave. The day I left was really hard. Rita, a novice I'd been a postulant with, was crying her eyes out and I was crying too. Sister Kathleen, this sour-faced bag of a nun, drove me to the airport with Rita in the back crying.

Looking back, there were relationships in the convent that were probably expressed sexually. Two sisters used to go away for weekends together. When Sister Mark came to stay with Sister Stanislaw, twice I saw her coming out of Stani's room in the morning, and Stani would just look at me and wink. She was a lovely person, a really beautiful woman; I mean, I could go back now and really enjoy it! It wasn't expressed in such an overt way so that the rest of the community knew about it, but you could certainly tell when one nun would spend more time with another nun. A convent is a world within a world, and what the outside world sees is very different to the actual nucleus of nuns as a group of women who work, pray and eat together. If you live that close to someone, then naturally it follows that closer relationships are going to build up, but it takes place within an almost secret world which is only now beginning to be acknowledged. But it's not the way it's portrayed in bloody porn films or the way that men see nuns doing it. When you're a novice you're watched almost day and night, but I think that if I'd reached the point where I was a professed sister then something would have happened. That's because what goes on between professed sisters is between you and your conscience, according to Catholic teaching.

I left on 21st December 1977 and I was twenty-two. I felt my whole world had stopped. One minute I was in a convent, the next I was off the plane in the middle of London feeling totally isolated. Perhaps I went to work at St Joseph's Hospice because it's run by nuns, and for a while I was following the same pattern. I was very confused at that point; I had a couple of boyfriends but I still felt the same disappointment. I had the view that sex was something that I should avoid as far as possible, because I was a higher spiritual being, and I suppose for a little while I could see myself going back into a convent. But I soon came down to earth with a bump. I'm not sure how it happened, I can't put my finger on it, but I was staying with my mum and dad and I began to think about relationships, and Mary. I had heard a few discussions on the radio about gays at this time, so I suppose it was in my head, and I just found myself saying the word lesbian and wondering if perhaps I was one. So I went into the front room and rang up Capital Helpline, who said the best thing was to talk to another lesbian. I rang up Lesbian Line. It's not their policy to meet women personally, but I told this woman my background and how confused I was and I met her on a Friday at the Embankment.

That was my first actual contact, my first encounter with a living, breathing dyke. It hit me at gut level . . . well, a bit lower actually. I was really aware of my sexual feelings for women and a little bit uncomfortable with them. There I was sitting in a busy Wimpy bar, and there was she saying the word lesbian quite loudly, rolling her own fags and being really positive. From that point I met her a few times and went to a few Lesbian Line meetings, but felt they were very much involved in their own internal politics, so my first contact with lesbian feminists wasn't a very positive one apart from Eileen. Also at that time, because I'd opened the floodgates a bit, there was a hell of a lot of negative as well as positive stuff, and it really hit me. This was just after my first sexual experience with a woman. I really enjoyed it and that's why I felt guilty. Before, I didn't have anything to feel guilty about because I hadn't enjoyed myself, and as a woman within the framework of Catholicism that was quite okay. But when I was getting to the point where I was thinking that I could like this, something inside me seemed to sabotage any positive feelings. It worked up over a couple of years to a point where it actually made me physically ill. It took me into deep depressions and made me agoraphobic.

I couldn't stay in the nurses' home because I'd had a fling with one of the staff nurses, so I left St Joseph's and landed up squatting round the Elephant & Castle. I started going to some of the pubs round south-east London like the Vauxhall Tavern, the White Bear, and the Crown, which were really heavy 'bar dyke' places. I was in a situation I didn't want to be in. I was tall and boyish so I got labelled butch. I used to go to the Crown in Blackfriars Road mostly. The butches and femmes would go there several nights a week. It was a world of extremes and the acting out of frustrations. The butches had these hideous suits that you get off the peg at C&A's and most of the femmes dressed like ultra stereotyped females. I found it a very violent, alcohol-ridden environment.

I originally lost my front teeth because a woman accused me of chatting up her bird. It was a mixed pub, us at one end and the heterosexuals at the other end. But because they were aping so much of heterosexuality in a way they were accepted. I had bad experiences, but I had a few novel experiences too. One time I landed up in the same bed with a butch and a femme and that's where I got the label 'versatile'. I did used to argue with the bar dykes and say there was no reason for having role-playing and that being a lesbian was about women loving women as women not as substitute husbands or wives, but it was obvious that they got a lot of security that way. I felt very numb in this scene, considering what was going on inside me. I wanted to be somewhere else but I felt stuck.

In many senses, although some of the experiences I went through were pretty horrendous, I needed to go through them. I entered the convent at seventeen and left at twenty-two, and they're very important years. In a convent you don't do a lot of emotional growing, so when I came out I had all these feelings that had to be lived out in some way. It was like a delayed adolescence, where you get hurt and screwed up if you want to expose yourself to finding out what it's all about. But these negative experiences all built up to give me the view that sex was disgusting and I was a degenerate sinner, and my body was a millstone round my spiritual neck. There was still a hell of a lot of Catholicism in me, and my way of showing my anger and disgust for my body was to throw myself against walls.

At around that time I got involved with a woman called Mary, who came out of the bar dyke scene. We both helped one another to get out of that particular environment, but I still found myself very depressed and guilty, I felt I couldn't do anything. It was obvious at that point that I had to do something otherwise I was going to have a complete breakdown, so I got the name of a lesbian Gestalt therapist, and I started going to see her. Slowly I began to work through all this negative guilt, to feel comfortable with myself as a person and a lesbian. That took quite a while, I had massive ups and downs and there were times when I completely went to pieces. I felt I couldn't cope with the physical act of sex, and I began to masturbate, which really helped in the sense that it gave me a more positive attitude to my body, which is a good base. It was mostly about working on feeling comfortable with myself and realizing that I wasn't a sinful person and that a big part of me was my lesbianism, and I had a right to express that. Mary and I were living together still but we'd stopped having a sexual relationship after the first year. At that time I still found it difficult to go out and I was unemployed and had very little money or motivation, but slowly I reached a point where I felt I wanted to live by myself. Up until then Mary and I had done everything together; it was a problem breaking away from that.

A year ago I met a woman called Jenny, and we both seemed to click. I felt consciously that I wanted an emotional and physical relationship with her and we had a whirlwind romance. I met her at a women's disco. I'd started going out a little bit, to a different kind of lesbian scene and was beginning to see positive images of lesbian feminists which did a lot to give me confidence, so sooner or later something was bound to happen. And it did. We must have spent the first couple of months in bed. I really enjoyed sex with Jenny. I enjoyed sex for itself, and for being in love with someone, and I didn't feel any guilt about it which gave me a real boost. Around this time I did six months work on a film unit as a security guard. The film was *Sacred Hearts*; it was about nuns and it was actually filmed in a convent. I really enjoyed that because it put me at ease with a lot of my feelings about nuns and convents.

When I entered the convent it was Donny Osmond; when I came out it was Sid Vicious. In 1973 it was clean-cut Americanism, and in '77 it was punk. It was aggression, it was anarchy, it was drugs, it was all types of sexual practices, it was black leather and chains: it was a hell of a shock to me. I wondered what my identity was; what was I? In the seventies you had a massive political awakening amongst young people, I did miss out on all of that. If I'd stayed in London perhaps I would have got in touch with all that and had a different story. Yet considering the type of person I was, a worse thing could have happened to me than going into a convent; I could have become a Catholic mother. I think I made the best choice, because I can't imagine trying to come out of a Catholic marriage. I think that besides whatever else I say, you do get positive images of women in convents; they're really strong, independent women and you hardly have any contact with men.

I suppose because of my particular history I'm reluctant to identify myself with one particular thing. I feel strongly about nuclear weapons but there is no way I could become totally immersed as a Greenham woman, because that would make me feel like when I was a nun and it would be like following a particular doctrine. I think I'm political in the way I live my life, not by what group meeting or demonstration I go to.

Looking back on all the experiences I've gone through, they've brought me to where I am now. I feel at ease with myself; I feel comfortable; I feel happy with what I've got. I feel happy about the relationship I've been through with Jenny and the two relationships I'm in at the moment. And I feel good about living on my own and being my own person. I'm not working, but I think that's out of choice which makes unemployment a lot more bearable. Basically now I want to go back to school and study for some A levels and see if I can do something like physiotherapy or osteopathy. So in a sense I feel as if I'm at the beginning again, as if I've got a fresh start and I no longer feel frightened about going out and being with other women and other dykes. I feel happy about the stage of life that I'm at.

POSTSCRIPT

I'm now working as a gardener for Lambeth Council. I wish I'd done this years ago. It's like a hobby and there's loads of variety. I've also had the opportunity to study because of it.

I'm in the third year of a relationship and we now live together with my lover's 13-year-old daughter and five cats and a dog. I don't imagine it'll always be the same but I'd like to stay with her for however long I've got. It comes as a shock to be living with this woman; it's not what I was thinking when I was interviewed, but you never know what comes around the corner.

I wanted to be in this book because if we don't put ourselves in history no one else will. I also want it to be known that no particular sort of woman is a lesbian, we have all kinds of backgrounds. Lastly I wanted to show that it's not all 'doom and gloom' – we can have very happy lives.

Megan Thomas, 21 May 1988

ZERRIN

INTERVIEWED ON 19 MARCH 1986 BY LIZ FLETCHER

I was born in Cyprus in a very small village in 1956. My memories of being a child are either very positive or very negative. In Cyprus I had a lot of freedom when I was young because my mother went out to work and my sister looked after us. I was allowed to play and climb trees and I would run wild. We lived in a village up to the age of six, then we moved to Limassol.

Most of the summer evenings people would sit outside under the jasmine trees. I remember one of the neighbours buying a television and inviting people round to watch it. We would sit in the garden, the television would be in the doorway, and you'd get loads of kids sitting in a row watching.

I remember not having hot water, so every time we wanted a bath we used to leave a big container of water outside and the sun would heat it up. In our garden – well, it was more like a backyard – we had an apple, a lemon, a date, and an almond tree, and I remember I was always a good climber. I could climb up but I would never be able to get down. I used to eat the dates when they were all green and horrible so we could make something with the pips like a necklace. I remember picking jasmines to make necklaces to sell, as that was the only way I was going to get any money to buy pencils and rubbers and things like that. We'd pick tiny little flowers in the early evening and by the time it was eight or nine o'clock they would have blossomed. We'd go over to the park and sell them. I used to always get into trouble for that because my mum thought that was begging.

I think that in 1963 the conflict began in Cyprus. The island wasn't divided then, but I remember having things drummed into

146

my head about not playing with the Greek children. We were told not to pick any fruits off the trees in case they were poisoned, and that they were trying to kill us. We still did it as it made it more exciting thinking that it was forbidden.

I started school at the age of six. The schools were very strict and getting things wrong meant you were going to get hit. The thing that stuck in my mind was the uniform: red and white gingham dresses which reminded me of the flag: its red background and white moon and star.

Around twice a year we had special days off, such as Ramadan. The children would celebrate it more because they'd actually go round visiting the elders getting sweets and money, and whenever Ramadan came round I'd have a new frock. Sometimes when you visited really poor and elderly people they'd say a prayer in front of you, and I thought, 'I don't want this, I want money.' You'd have a competition: who could get the most money, pennies really. You'd be visiting very early in the morning about half-past five. Sometimes if it were a certain festival we'd have henna on our hands. My mother would put it on her hair but I wasn't allowed to because I wasn't a woman. I could have it on my hand and maybe I'd have a moon and star. They would call me a woman as soon as I started my period. Mind you, when I did start it I got a slap in the face. I don't know why. Speaking to other Turkish girls I found that their mums slapped their face as well. I thought, 'Is this my fate for being a girl?'

I remember periods being quite negative and being told to shave. In England I was given a razor blade and told to go to the bathroom to shave. I never talked to my eldest sister about it, because of the way we'd been brought up. Periods and sex were things you didn't talk about. I didn't know what sex was. We didn't have sex education and I didn't know where babies came from. I remember giggling when watching films and seeing couples kissing. I remember going under my bed and doing the same things with a friend, you know, kissing. They're my first memories of physical contact. I remember saying to my friend that when I had a baby she would be allowed to feed it and I would breastfeed her baby. In some way I thought that would make them sisters and quite close: I'd seen other women doing it. When I was born my mum said that, because she had to go out to work, the neighbour would feed me because they were having babies at the same time. That was done a lot at the time. You didn't do it for money, you looked after each other's children as a way of supporting each other.

I felt everything that I learned came through women and I remember my looking up to how strong they were. I used to think there was this burden on us, that because we were born female we were inferior, but at the same time I saw strong women around me. I saw my mother going out to work from half-past five, so to me she wasn't weak, she was the breadwinner.

I think around that time I started asking my mum, 'Why do boys get treated differently?' She would say, 'Because they are boys.' She'd make no secret about it, that because they were boys they were stronger. What would I be doing? I'd be getting an arranged marriage and having children. The only thing I had to do was to have children and to learn how to knit and sew and make dresses. That would be it.

Q: *You've touched on the positive aspects, perhaps now you could say something about the bad times?*

I don't mind. For years I didn't talk about the negative experiences in my childhood. I had been silenced. I think the most disturbing thing that ever happened to me was incest, and it wasn't until five years ago that I actually started talking about it. I don't mind talking now as I feel it helps me and it may help other women.

It started when I was six. I don't really remember what was happening to me, because as far as I was concerned all fathers might be like that. I thought because he wasn't a stranger it meant that it was OK. I didn't really think about it then, but when I was eleven I remember feeling quite powerless. I didn't want this thing to carry on but it was still happening to me. It wasn't so much that I consented to it, rather it was that I didn't have the power to stop it. I couldn't talk to my mother.

I remember an incident that happened when I was about ten and my mother going mad and having a big argument because my father tried to do it to a neighbour's daughter. She really hit the roof. I remember thinking, 'Why don't you do something about it happening to me? Why go mad because it happened to a stranger? I'm your daughter.' But I couldn't really say it to her because as far as I was concerned my mum loved me. I remember when it actually came out into the open she started locking the bedroom door, and around that time she started planning to leave Cyprus. It was her way of escaping. She had the power then because she had a British passport and he didn't. She worked for the British at an army base. I think it took two years before she had enough money to pay for the fares for all of us. I think that was one of the most wonderful moments of my life, being told that we'd be leaving in August. This was 1968.

I remember seeing my father off at the harbour. I was really happy. I remember my mum saying, 'Give him a last kiss', and I thought, 'No, I don't want to kiss him', and I remember seeing tears in his eyes. I felt nothing. The community felt sorry for him because he was going to be left without any family, but I didn't. I knew why and my mum knew why and I admired her because she had made the decision to leave.

I remember in the boat I was so sick but persevering because it would be alright once I got here. We ended up in Dover, then we got a train to Victoria. My uncle came to pick us up. I imagined he would have a massive house, but it was two-storey with one family living at the bottom. It was rather shocking to me that housing conditions were so bad: damp walls, a horrible floor and kitchen. It wasn't at all what I'd imagined it to be. I'd imagined it to be a really beautiful house with a beautiful garden, because back in Cyprus, when I went to visit my mum at work, all the British lived in beautiful houses with carpets and had green gardens. So it was quite a shock to find some British people living in poverty. This was Battersea. We didn't live there long. I didn't go to school there because we moved to Forest Hill. My mum got this job finishing off garments and my sister worked in the same factory, sewing, and my brother, pressing clothes. They told me I was lucky because I was going to make it to school, a white British school.

I remember my first day at school, being introduced to another girl who was Turkish, but she didn't look Turkish to me. They said she would take care of me because I couldn't speak English. This girl really didn't want to be lumbered with me. I was determined to learn. I wasn't going to be dependent on this girl.

Once I spoke English I found it easy to make friends. I started mixing with lots of Black girls in the school and there were a few times when they said, 'how come you can't speak English properly and we can and we're Black?' They were the same colour as me and I felt, this is where I belong. But then there was the culture difference between us, as they were mostly born over here and I didn't feel English. I think there was a point in my life when I started denying that I was Turkish Cypriot. I actually said I was British because I could speak English and there was no way you might guess that I was Turkish Cypriot. I said I was a Black girl born here.

There were some staff who said we were lucky to be there getting an education as where we came from we might not have the chance. I remember being told that we smell and we were dirty; this came mostly from white girls in the school.

I just couldn't wait to leave school. I wasn't encouraged, nobody actually said to me, 'Listen, you're like this because of the language barrier and not because you're thick', as I sat exams but didn't get anything. I didn't even go to see the Careers Service. The option I had was going into the factory because my family was there and I'd be quite safe amongst the Turkish community. I rebelled against that, and although I still feel I didn't have a good choice I went into an office to do filing. I found that really boring.

One of the things I did was to have my hair short. I wanted to be grown-up and I started plucking my eyebrows and wearing make-up. My mum didn't mind that, but she minded me wearing mini-skirts as I was a Muslim girl and she didn't want me to wear tight trousers as they showed off my figure. I started asking for freedom to go out with my friends to discos. I remember being beaten up by my brother because I asked to go to a disco. I remember my mother nagging at him to take me out but he used to say, 'No, I'm not dragging her along with me.' I think that was one of the reasons I thought about marriage as an option to get out.

My family had mentioned that I was coming up to an age where they would be thinking about arranged marriages, because sixteen, to them, is quite a good age to get married. I was told that soon people would be coming just to meet me and I would be expected to behave in a certain manner, sit there like a lady and after fifteen minutes get up and make the tea without them telling me to. They told me I was not to look at the boy too much. I would make the tea and bring it in on a tray and start offering it to the eldest one in the room – that didn't include my mother – and end with the boy. I wasn't to look at him or smile or laugh because that meant I wasn't a good girl. That never did happen, as I didn't see why I should go through all that. As far as I was concerned I was capable of arranging my own life whether it meant going out to find him, but I wasn't going to have someone tell me this was the guy I was going to marry and actually say to someone, 'Come and look at me and buy me'. I didn't tell them that, though. I just said, 'Yeah, maybe you're right, but not yet.' The only excuse I could give was that I wanted to work a bit more and buy more clothes before I got married.

I'd met this boy who lived in the same street and I was quite friendly with him, so rather than them arrange a marriage, I thought, 'There's someone that actually likes me' and I liked him, so I started sneaking out with him and not going to work sometimes, and told mum that I was working overtime when I was meeting him. He was Asian and seventeen. I think all I wanted was freedom. I didn't really want to get married but when they found out about us, they were either going to stop me from seeing him or make me marry someone else. My mother asked if we'd been sleeping together and I said, 'No.' She said, 'You'd better tell the truth', or my brothers would take me to the doctors to have a test to see whether I was a virgin or not. At that time I *had* started sleeping with him. I was sixteen and really scared. Two days later I ran away with him because I thought they might find out.

We were on our way to Gretna Green but never made it. We got to North London where we had some friends. We decided to stay there for a week. He phoned his parents and they said, 'Come back, come and live here: she can live here too.' I actually lived there for a couple of months without being married but we weren't allowed to sleep together. After a couple of months I went through a ceremony where I had a Muslim marriage, and then I had to go to the registry office and get married again, as a Muslim marriage didn't really count in this country.

When I got married I was three months pregnant. I lived with his parents. I'd have done anything not to be sent back home so I was under their thumb. My relationship with his parents wasn't that close because I couldn't speak Bengali and they couldn't speak English well. They owned a restaurant so were away most nights. It wasn't until I'd actually had the baby and was going to the restaurant to give them a hand that I became closer to them. They were really happy because the baby was a boy, the first born a boy. After having my first child I got pregnant again after two months and had another boy.

After four years I wanted us to live on our own. I don't think I actually ever enjoyed being married. I spent all four years really working. I used to feel exhausted and I had no social life. We were still without any kind of money and independence because he was studying and I was not earning any money, so we applied for a council house. We got a place but after three weeks he'd left and gone back to his mum. He didn't want to be married anymore. I realized I wasn't ready for marriage but I wasn't going to walk out because I had two children and there was no way I could leave them. I had my pride and wasn't going to follow him around. It didn't work, so I was going to prove that I could survive on my own. I was twenty.

I'd patched up the relationship with my mum, thank God, because she was really supportive. I thought she would say to me, 'Look you made your own bed, you lie in it; I didn't ask you to marry him.' I lived on my own for a year, then went to live with my mum. I was accepted back into the home. I still feel that it's through this that I've got quite close to her, because she'd actually been divorced twice and had two young kids. We had this in common. At that time everyone had married so there was just me and her and my two children. By this time mum had retired so she looked after the children and I went to work in a factory.

When I was twenty-two I had a relationship with a woman. While I was going to work I started socializing and going out. The first time that I actually went into a pub I met a woman there, and we started off by being friends and got closer. My mum went back to Cyprus for a holiday and this woman came round to stay and we just started a relationship. We didn't talk about it, we just started doing it: it wasn't a big issue. I think that after three months I felt really guilty that I was actually having this relationship with a woman. I felt that if I was ever found out I'd be in disgrace. If the social workers ever found out my kids would be taken away and I felt really afraid that my kids may discover. So

152

I told this woman that I wasn't a lesbian, that I could be bisexual, but I wasn't a lesbian because I'd been married. I told her to go. I told her that I was sorry but I didn't want to see her, and I even told her that I might go back to my husband.

I spent the next five years celibate thinking, 'Am I a lesbian, am I not?' I was really confused, because as far as I was concerned I didn't *have* sexuality. For five years I felt, well, I definitely wasn't heterosexual, but was I a lesbian? I also felt that because I'd spent four years being married I couldn't possibly be a lesbian.

Around that time, 1979, I started being quite active in women's groups. It was a women's health group and wasn't political as such. It wasn't that the word sexuality was never used, but it was about relationships with men all the time, straight sex. I mentioned that I'd not had a relationship since I got divorced and it was looked on as something wrong. People would say that you need to lose weight, that's why you're not going out to meet men. You haven't got the confidence in yourself. But I knew I wasn't shy. It was because I didn't want a relationship. I never dared open my mouth and say I'd had a relationship with a woman.

I wanted at one time to talk about incest, but there's no way I was going to open a discussion because I didn't want them to think, 'She's an incest survivor', and expose myself. I wanted everyone to be concerned about the issue. Most of my friends were women and straight. Some of them were really racist. They always said to me, 'You're not Black, you're not like the rest of them', trying to console me.

When I started to be active, helping women and migrant people to claim benefits, they used to say to me, 'If they don't like it here they should go back home and not come and get money from us.' I never used to challenge this as they were friends, and although they were racist I did have support from them, like there were times when I didn't have any money and they would give or loan money to me. So I felt really obliged. I didn't dare say, 'Look, that isn't fair what you're saying: you're being racist.'

About 1982 I set up a Turkish women's group while I was attending other groups like photography and women's drama. I decided that all those other groups weren't catering for women from other backgrounds. They were mostly set up by white women and attended by white women. I knew many Turkish women living on the estate and thought there was a point where they could come together. Three or four years ago, for Turkish women to organize separately was quite a task as it meant that you had to get permission from their men before they could attend a women's group.

There were around twelve women between the ages of eighteen and sixty. A Turkish Women's Day that followed was organized by myself, the Turkish women, and some of the community workers on the estate. It was well attended by about fifty women, but I was thinking to myself, there's about forty white women (although at that time I called them English) and ten Turkish women. I wanted it to be the other way round, but I think we were lucky to get ten Turkish women there. When our group met we would discuss things like our position in this country as second-class citizens. We'd talk about the difficulties in getting benefit, anything.

Q: *Did you ever discuss lesbianism?*

No. God! No way. Although I didn't use the word feminism I was actually becoming quite a radical feminist, and I took on issues like Greenham. I started visiting Greenham and started talking about artificial insemination by donor. I was saying there were other ways of having babies, you could choose alternative ways, but never quite saying there are lesbian women who could start a family if they wanted to. I don't know how that would have gone down, I probably would have got stoned to death.

I started talking to the white workers on the estate about sexuality. I was visiting Greenham, 1983–4, and many of the women I was friends with kept saying to me that at Greenham they were all lesbians and I mustn't go because I would be affected. I kept saying, 'Look, what makes you think I'm not a lesbian now?' and they said, 'Of course you're not; you're a victim of circumstances, looking for somewhere to belong.'

It was in the Greenham group and at Greenham that I met lots of lesbians. I came out to a man at one of the user groups on the estate and he was quite supportive. My friend started crying and said I was lying; she couldn't accept the fact that I was a lesbian. Another woman that I'd been quite close to said it was just something I was going through and I'd just been unlucky with men. I told them I'd had a relationship when I was twenty-two but they didn't believe me. This time I was ready. I was going to be quite open about it and if they didn't like me that was their problem. I was still the same person, I just preferred women. They kept saying, 'What would your boys think of you?' and it wouldn't be fair on them. They were nine and ten. I said, 'It wouldn't be fair on me if I hid it until they left home; I'd be deny-ing myself so much and I've denied myself six years anyway.' So I started openly saying I was a lesbian. People kept saying to me, 'You're not having a relationship with a woman, so how can you be a lesbian?' They couldn't understand.

I think it wasn't until I got to Greenham that I actually realized that I had a sexuality. I could talk about whatever I wanted to talk about and I started talking about being an incest survivor and felt that I wasn't the only one. There were so many around me being so close to other women that it just felt the right thing to do. Greenham gave me a lot of courage to openly say that I was a lesbian. Nobody was going to say, well you're not having a relationship, because there were so many lesbians there not in a relationship. However, I wasn't not with a woman out of choice or politics but because I was quite shy and I wasn't going to make the first attempt to sleep with somebody. I was looking at women and finding them attractive but there was no way I was going to make the first move. I felt that if I found the right woman I would have gone ahead.

I started going to lots of women's socials and clubs and getting into the scene. After a while I had a relationship with a woman and then I met the woman who I first went with. I hadn't seen her for five years or so and I started seeing her again. The relationship didn't last long though; I'd moved on and she didn't have any political interest at all so we split up.

I've now been having a relationship with my lover for the last ten months, but we've been friends for two years. I think I was looking for someone to fall in love with, and I wanted her to be someone who would actually understand where I was coming from and had gone through something like I had, someone that didn't have it easy. Both of us are incest survivors so I can freely talk about it to her and she can talk to me. I feel it's really important for us to have a relationship, a good friendship whether we're lovers or not, because of so much we share together. My children know; they've accepted it but I still feel there's a long way to go because they are boys and I'm doing my best to bring them up in a way so they don't oppress women. I know they're never going to be proud of me for being a lesbian, but they accept the situation. They get involved in our conversations and in our arguments. They know about sexism and racism. They accept my relationship with my lovers, although sometimes I feel there is jealousy between them and I get stuck in the middle. I wish that my sons would grow up with the possibility of having an option about their sexuality. I live in a women's housing co-op, so that's good for two boys to be living around and learning from women.

Although at times I still organize with white women I feel the need to organize separately with Black women because there are certain things we can discuss. I'm involved in the co-op so I think that's all I can manage at the moment, having a full-time job, two children and a relationship.

A group of us started a lesbian group for Turkish women two weeks ago and now there's eight of us. I mean at one time I used to think I was the only one, the only Turkish Cypriot lesbian. I feel I've achieved a lot, I've moved a lot.

POSTSCRIPT

It was important for me to do this interview. I feel that I have contributed to lesbian history and the anthology will show that it is not just a white history and will shatter the myths about lesbianism and motherhood.

My children, thirteen and fourteen, now live with their father during the week. I faced the fact that he had a responsibility towards them and I needed the space to think about my life. I had to understand that this was not selfish and irresponsible, as I have been made to feel by 'society'. In fact, this move has allowed me and the boys to enjoy each other more.

I now use my birth name and not the English name I took on. I've reached a point where I know who I am and I am no longer willing to compromise. I am proud to be a Turkish Cypriot lesbian mother.

Zerrin, March 1988

156

AQUEELA

INTERVIEWED ON 22 FEBRUARY 1986 BY
ALLEGRA DAMJI

I was born in the Indian Maternity home in Nairobi, Kenya, in August 1957. My memories of the first eight years of my life are a mixture of a few colourful picnics at Nairobi City Park and the hustle bustle of living next door to one of the busiest Indian cinemas in Nairobi, the Liberty, which played films like *Ali Baba Chali Chore* [Ali Baba and the Forty Thieves]. Though we lived in quite a few areas of Nairobi, according to my mother, my strongest memories are of the flat next to the Liberty.

When I was eight my father died. I remember it very vividly. People say I was his favourite but I don't know what that's supposed to mean. My mother was coming to England to visit her parents with my brother and little sister, and I was staying with my father and his cousins in Kisumo, which is a few hundred miles away from Nairobi. I was left with the cousins while my father drove the rest of the family back to Nairobi so they could fly out. On that journey he stopped to have tea in Kericho, which is famous for its tea, and he died of a heart attack. He was forty-two and my mum was twenty years younger than him.

I remember driving along in a car with my aunt, and one of my cousins stopping the car on the side of the road and saying in gestures that Hamifi had died and being hush-hush because I was in the car. I picked it up straight away, even though they thought I couldn't understand. I remember just crying the whole time and people buying me crisps and chocolates to stop me, but I wouldn't because I knew and just wanted someone to say:

When we reached home there was my mother, and my father's

157

body was lying all covered-up ready for the funeral, and that's the first time adults actually acknowledged that he had died. That was after a twenty-four-hour-long journey back to Nairobi. I can remember my father's shroud being purple. We have white shrouds, but there was a purple velvet cloth covering him and I had on a light-green-and-white checked dress. My mother, of course, dressed in white. Women are not allowed to go to the actual burial so the funeral was basically loads of people in our house. You mourn for forty days and the bereaved don't do any work, other people do it for you and you just sit there and talk about the person that's died. I have memories of all these people talking to my mother about my father but not to me. My uncles came round and asked if I wanted to do this or that but I said, 'No, I want to be here.' People just wouldn't talk to me about it. Mother did a bit initially but she was very, very distressed.

The marriage had been arranged and she didn't want to get married. She wanted to become a doctor but she was the eldest girl and her parents couldn't afford to keep four other kids after they got to a certain age. So she was married off very reluctantly, and in some ways she is still bitter about that. But I think they had a good marriage given those circumstances. She mourned his death for nine years. She dressed in black or white and wouldn't go to films or any big fun occasions: when my father was alive they used to go even though they were Muslims.

It was very difficult for her to bring up three kids on her own so she sent me – as I was the oldest one – to be looked after by my grandparents in England. In some ways that had a detrimental effect on me later when I began to feel resentful about being the one who was sent here. Their life out there always seemed so much better from the letters I got. They'd be talking about sunshine and sea and I was living in a country where it was too cold to go out to play. I remember being very envious of them.

I was very disappointed the day I came to England. I thought it would all be skating to school with little red woollies and coats with fur. When I saw how grey and ugly it looked, it wasn't the images I had which were more like bits of Switzerland: a fairytale land.

My grandparents lived in a flat in Wandsworth. I loved them both dearly and both enriched my life in their own way. My grandmother insisted on me acquiring practical skills, and passed on to me all the ones she had. By the age of ten I could sew, cook and decorate. I was not always a willing learner and would often rebel, but my grandmother was an equally forceful women and she often won. She used to say it was important for me to learn to do everything because I was going to have to survive on my own. I don't know what she meant by this unless she had some premonition of my life to come. I wish she was alive now because I'd really thank her for it but at the time I thought she was wicked.

My grandad was amazing; he was trained as a Muslim priest but he never practised for very long. He was very gentle, thoughtful; a philosopher in lots of ways. I remember talking to him about Communism, Marxism, and Islam. This was all after prayers at six in the morning before I went to school. He bought me sweets which my grandmother barred him from doing. He had a very sweet tooth himself; we were like two naughty kids. She'd hate sending us shopping because we'd buy the wrong things. He was an old man when I knew him and he was eighty-five when he died. He taught me the Koran. I had to recite it every day after school, which I hated. Now I'm glad I can read Arabic.

In Nairobi we spoke Swahili and Punjabi. We were also taught English early on because Kenya was still a colony when I was a kid. I spoke English quite fluently. At home we spoke a mixture of Punjabi and Swahili, and Urdu which was seen as a more genteel language for little girls to learn. But I was very stubborn and spoke Punjabi, which my grandfather said always sounds like you're arguing even if you're not. Genteelness was never in my nature. Urdu is a very beautiful language but I didn't like all the gentility surrounding it. So I was brought up a very multilingual kid. We learnt Swahili as the main language of East Africa, Punjabi as our own language, and Urdu because of our Muslim connections.

In Britain I didn't have much to do with the Asian community. There weren't any Asian kids in my school. I was part of it in the sense of that's how we socialized, but as a teenager I rejected all that. I saw myself as above it. The fact that I was one of them was beside the point. The experience of racism made me deny my own culture. Paki-bashing was a very real threat when I was going to school. My uncles were coming home bleeding after being in fights with skinheads. Especially on darker mornings when I had to walk to school it felt frightening.

At school I would deny being Asian. Fear led me to clutch at anything for safety: I deluded myself and thought by not mixing with my own community, by drinking coffee instead of tea, I would somehow be safe, more acceptable, not so 'native'. At the same time I would fight back if I was abused. Once the cookery teacher made us make Spaghetti Bolognaise, and I put spices in it and she told me not to. I said 'This is what my grandparents are eating tonight and we want spices in it.' She ended up telling me to go home in a banana boat. Two Afro-Caribbean girls who were at the school said they respected me for that, because they didn't think us 'Pakis' were strong enough to fight back. We became friends.

At fourteen I got very politically involved and joined things like the Students Action Union, the Angela Davies Campaign, and the Young Communist League. Reflecting back on it now I would say I developed what I'd call a pseudo-Black consciousness. We were still very Westernized but we were not going to be abused for not being white. I remember talking to an assembly about the Soledad Brothers. The headmistress, Dame Margaret Miles, said that it had been very good but she had one correction to make: that he hadn't been murdered in prison but shot while trying to escape. I got very angry and organized a Black girls' demo to stage a sit-in outside her office. I got suspended.

I have pretty good memories of school. Some of my teachers really liked me but I didn't do well. I came out with two O levels. I always wanted to be a lawyer. I have regrets now and think if I went back now I'd keep my head down and not fight so much. But that's easy to say. I didn't like being abused and getting called a Paki. I thought of myself as Punjabi, Kenyan. At school they used to talk about the slave trade and primitive jungles, when Africa was being discussed. Nairobi is a huge city with the biggest Hilton Hotel in the world. But at school I was being told about how Africa was mud huts and wild animals. My grandfather was pretty sussed but he thought I should just work hard and be somebody, because nobody would listen to me until then. Which in some ways is true, but in others . . . What is a somebody? I'm not nobody.

Sex was never talked about in our family. From when I was nine until I was about fifteen I was sexually abused by my uncle. It was very painful and frightening. I remember being in my room and being really scared because I knew my uncle would be coming up. I've been very hesitant about talking about it until this last year because I never wanted people to think of that experience as a reason for my lesbianism. As far as I'm concerned, that's a load of crap! Given that the percentage of incest victims is something like 70 per cent of the female population, then why aren't they all dykes? [laughs] It would be rather nice if they were. I didn't tell my mother because I didn't want her to feel guilty. She feels guilty enough for having sent me to England because I haven't turned out the way a good Muslim girl should. I protected my family from it for years, and later on it became a matter of proving to myself that it hadn't affected me. I went through numerous relationships with men to prove that I was 'normal'. Rather than that being what I wanted sexually. Now I think the incest *has* affected me, and probably will for the rest of my life, but I hasten to add that my life is a positive one. My uncle ended up in a mental home and I don't particularly want him out. I have no sympathy for him. He was violent to his wife and his daughter went into care, so I feel it's not only me he's hurt.

When I was sixteen my mum came to England and I went to live with her for a year. We didn't get on well at all because I was a politico and wanted to go to all these meetings, and mum didn't like that. So I ran away. While she was at work one day I phoned up the Samaritans and said I was homeless and they sent me to Centrepoint. I was seventeen and a half. I stayed three nights and helped the workers and ended up getting a job in a homeless girls' hostel. That's how I got into social work.

Ninety-nine per cent of the time I hated sleeping with men, but I did have one relationship with a man who I cared about a lot. He was about twenty years older than me and kept asking me to marry him. The main reason I didn't settle down with him was because I didn't think my mum could cope with me coming home with an older white man, or any white man.

Eventually I went to Paris to get away from him and think about what I wanted next, and it was there that I met this woman. I was sitting in a café wearing a feminist badge, and this woman had one on too and she came over to talk to me. When I replied in perfect English she nearly died of shock. She was speaking in Pidgin. We became really good friends and spent a lot of time with each other. She lived on the Left Bank which was near all the trendy nightspots, so we'd go out and come home at three in the morning and we'd always stay at her place. That was fine, no problem at all, until one day she told me she was a dyke! [laughs] After that I slept on the floor for a few weeks and then we talked about it more openly and I got less frightened. Then one night we just slept together. And that bloomed into a beautiful relationship which lasted for the year before we came back to this country. We still love each other terribly. That was my first lesbian experience.

In Paris I identified as a lesbian but when I came back to London I did have a brief relationship with a man. That was partly because of the reactions I got from friends. The first person that I told was my flatmate, who I got on with very well. She came to visit me in Paris. I remember that I had decided that there was no way I was going to hide Marie away for the weekend. So I told her at the airport and she burst into tears. Her mother was a lesbian who lived with this other woman who had been through a sex change operation. I felt very bad about upsetting her, but it was a really important part of my life and something I wasn't going to hide. I wanted her to meet Marie and I felt that, once she had, she'd like her so much it would make the world of difference [laughs]. Was I being starry-eyed? She did meet her and reluctantly liked her, but her attitude was that it was just a phase I was going through.

Soon after I came back to England and I had a birthday party and that was chaos. I'd invited all my new-found friends from Women's Aid, and all my men friends found it terribly threatening and were really rude to Marie – apart from my best-friend Wilf, who brought a bottle of vodka and took me and Marie upstairs and we sat and talked and ignored the party downstairs. He was a Black guy and he and we sat talking about how we got into social work and what it was like being Black in an almost all-white crowd. I have very fond memories of that. I've never actually talked to Wilf about my lesbian relationships, I just said, 'Well, I'm a lesbian and I'm going out with this woman and I'm very happy.' Which I think he was pretty pleased about because he didn't like my last boyfriend. He thought he was too old for me and used to call him 'rat features' [laughs].

So I came back and I suppose I was making this big statement about being a dyke, and I was quite astonished at the reaction I got. My friends and I were very close in that we were all lefties together. We were involved in Rock Against Racism, and we used to go to Chapel Market every Saturday and Sunday mornings to demonstrate against the Fascists and get beaten up together, which makes you close. But their reaction to lesbianism was appalling. They totally ignored Marie and treated me like I was going through a phase. To this day she hates coming down to London because of the memory of that. But after she went home I missed my friends. I was fairly dependent on them. So I had one last flingette with a very nice boy.

He was more aware about sexual politics than my socialist friends. He'd read *The Female Eunuch* [laughs] and Kate Millet. He was the guy who told me about *Sita* because I told him about my doubts about heterosexuality. Now I think, 'Oh God, he must have really got off on that', because it's a terrible book. He thought it would be nice to go out with a bisexual [laughs]. He was a bit of a wimp really. So I finally packed that up. Poor bloke got kicked out in a blizzard at six o'clock in the morning. I remember kicking him out and thinking, 'Thank God he's gone, now I can have some peace'. But it had snowed really heavily and he couldn't move his motorbike. He came back upstairs five minutes later and asked if he could stay because it was snowed in and I said 'Don't talk rubbish, fuck off!' Not stirring out of bed to check it. So the poor guy went. Next day I discovered he was right [laughs]. Anyway, he survived.

After that I tried finding lesbians in London, but it was very hard. I used to go outside of London to see Marie a lot. We still slept with each other: we do now, occasionally, nine years later. It never occurred to me to ring Lesbian Line and I couldn't go to a disco on my own. I often wonder how women coming out *find* other women. So I do make an effort when I go into bars and I see a woman on her own, to say hello. It took me years to get to know other lesbians in London. I started joining a lot of women's groups where everybody was questioning their sexuality, except I knew I was a lesbian. I used to sit through these groups and say, 'Yeah, I'm questioning my sexuality' [laughs], thinking, I'm not but I'm just dying to meet another lesbian. Once I went with this group of straight socialist feminists to The Carved Red Lion, because they thought it was wonderful to go to a women's club. I really liked it and wanted to go without them [laughs]. Then a friend of mine from the old socialist days looked me up and I was saying how hard it was to meet other dykes. She told me that her sister Jerry was a dyke so I met her and we began clubbing together. I started meeting other dykes through that. Now I know loads. You need a way to get in on the crowds. It's really hard.

Nobody in my family knew about me being lesbian for a long time. I told my aunt about two years ago. Her reaction was wonderful. We were out to dinner and she said, 'You haven't mentioned boyfriends for years, whatever happened to that guy you went out with?' and I said 'Well, aunt, I'm a lesbian.' She said, 'Oh well, I know that.' Now she talks about it a lot and if anybody says anything anti-gay she really jumps down their throat. It's nice to have somebody in the family who knows. She came to the 'We are Here' Black women's conference with me, and she cooked for the Black lesbian conference. She's an amazing woman. Both my grandparents are dead and I would never tell my mother. She's become a stricter Muslim than she was when she was younger, and she feels it's her responsibility to keep the family culture and religion alive. She has taken on very traditional values so it would be very hard to communicate with her about it and I don't want to add to her guilt.

When I came back from France I decided to try and get a degree, so I went to North London Polytechnic to do an Applied Sciences course. I hated it. It was full of SWP [Socialist Workers' Party] politics, which I'd grown out of. There were only two Black lesbians in the whole college and by that time I had begun to question racism in the Women's Movement. A couple of the lecturers were well-known lesbians and they always looked on us as being the perfect models of sussed out Black lesbianism. I felt we were used. The Black students couldn't cope with our lesbianism and the white ones weren't interested in racism. Me and Beverley, the other Black lesbian, were left in limbo. We were really isolated.

Beverley committed suicide after the first two years [pause] and I left. It's difficult to describe how hard it was, and I'm still very angry. I was twenty-five when I went. I didn't have any qualifications but I'd been working in kids' homes. My politics were quite sorted out. I remember the disappointment with some lecturers whose books I'd read. One wrote on an essay of mine that I was very good on 'Blacks and women', and I was furious because I just felt she can't have read anything by Black women. You know: we're *Black women*. That was precisely the sort of racism in the

Women's Movement that Beverley Smith and Audre Lorde were challenging.

I was very upset by Beverley's death. I was on holiday in Spain for four weeks when she died and I really hated myself for not being here. I had begun to be involved with Black lesbian politics, but that was all very new. Beverley was always a hard studier – she got a First – and she didn't use the time at college in the same way as me. I was meeting other Black women, but she was totally isolated. She was a lesbian first and had felt very let down by the white lesbians. It was the Black lesbians I met who saw me though the devastation of her death. To this day I can't ask the white lesbians at college about Beverley's death. I think she took an overdose, but they are the only ones who can tell me. All those white women treated the group like it was a big dykes' party. They were into drinking and sleeping around. Their idea of feminism or activism was Greenham Common. Anything to do with Black people, like demonstrations against racist attacks or the invasion of Grenada, didn't interest them. These things were really important to me and Beverley, and we would argue about pacifism and the fact that in South Africa people can't afford to be all 'make love not war'. I felt that they had the luxury of being able to close their eyes to racism and that I didn't. About that time my brother was knifed in the cheek by some skinheads. I just felt these women were in a privileged position and did not use it to try to change anything. I don't mean 'don't have fun' but it's just what I call total drunken debauchery, which sounds like moralism but you would have to see it to believe it, really.

Recently I've been thinking about my own radicalism. It's hard, because I don't think it's something peculiar to me. I feel every woman can become a feminist; every woman has the capacity within herself to become independent. Whether she gets the chance is a different matter. I became an activist because I was angry about so many things – even at fourteen – and just felt I had to do something about it. I was angry about living in Britain because I had no choice about it. My origins lie in India and Pakistan, my mother was Indian but her family come from Pakistan, so I can't relate to any one country as far as India is concerned. I can't live in Kenya because it's an African country and Asians are not necessarily welcome there, because under colonialism Asians were pseudo-middle classes in those countries.

165

Also I've got a British passport, which I had no choice about as our family had to take out British citizenship in order to go and work in Kenya. They were starving in India because the colonial system encouraged private land-ownership and money-lending. Many Asians moved all over the world as cheap labour. My grandfather didn't agree with partition: he felt it should be Hindustan not Pakistan or Bangladesh. So I had his influence too. When I was told by skinheads to go back to my own country, where could I go? I still don't see this country as home. I have a need to identify with a Black country as a way of survival. If I walk down the street and someone says, 'Paki, go home!' I feel like saying, 'Fuck off! Who wants to live in your filthy, grey country anyway. You should see where I come from, it's paradise.' I know I have a right to live here but I need to be able to say that.

Now I'm an Asian girls' worker. There are lots of stereotypes about Asian girls. They are seen as passive and it's thought to be pointless giving them careers because they will just go off and marry. Afro-Caribbean girls are seen as aggressive, thieving and lazy. Now, in the Black Women's Movement, instead of saying, 'We're all Black and we're going to fight you together', we say, 'We're all Black but there are different types of racism. It affects our communities differently.'

Because I work with young women I can't be out openly, and that's very hard. In the project I work with we are all out to each other but not to the outside agencies we work with. It comes up all the time when you are working with young people, as gays are always mentioned as child abusers. Of course, the reality is that girls are abused by heterosexual men. I resent it because I have nothing to hide or be ashamed of.

Being a lesbian has made me feel powerful and that I don't have to compromise in my personal life anymore. I knew the times when men were being sexist as lovers, but for the sake of the relationship I didn't always say anything, but now I can go beyond all that. I became a lesbian through choice, but now the thought of sleeping with a man makes me feel sick, so it doesn't feel like a choice any longer. I don't want it to be anymore. It's a positive thing. I like sex with women, I like being with women and I like living as a lesbian.

Recently I went to the International Feminist Conference in Nairobi, which was absolutely amazing. I've never seen so many beautiful women together in my whole life [laughs]. So, apart from the eyes popping, it was amazing to see so many women from so many countries together. We went to the unofficial United Nations conference and there was an estimated 14,000 women there. Sometimes I wished I wasn't British. Feminism in this country has become so stale, but in other countries it is still fresh. Indian women were talking about all the fights against dowry which include direct action, which is what we miss in this country. I was talking to one women who told me how this girl in Bombay had been raped and all these women had demonstrated outside the rapist's house. It took the case two years to get to court but they virtually forced him to leave the area and made his life hell. There is nothing stopping us having demonstrations when we know of men who have raped or committed incest. At Great Ormond Street Children's Hospital it is recommended that the father has therapy and family be kept together. We could take action about that.

I believe in change. If I didn't I would just curl up and die. I don't think feminists will overturn Thatcher's Britain tomorrow, but feminists in the past have created equal opportunities and effected changes for women like me. I had no qualifications. I'm a Black woman. If people hadn't fought for equal opportunities I wouldn't have a job now. So to give up would mean that young women wouldn't have the same chance in the future. I have consoled myself by being satisfied with small changes. The other day I won a battle in a school so that Asian girls could sew trousers in their needlework class instead of the usual skirts, because they don't wear them. It would be terribly sad if everybody felt they couldn't change anything, because younger women would be going through exactly the same thing and by the time they were in their thirties be clapped out and ready to throw in the towel. And why should that happen? As far as I'm concerned it's a future investment. The more I fight now the less I'm going to have to fight in the future. Part of the reason for that is that I want to see other Asian women dare to have a future. I don't want there to be just five of us in a few years time. I want there to be twenty of us, because we'll be that much stronger.

Islington, London, 1988. Portrait by Nicky West

JOYCE McFARLANE

INTERVIEWED ON 8 JUNE 1987 BY ALLEGRA DAMJI

I was born on February 19th, 1959, at City Hospital, Nottingham, and brought up by my mother and stepfather until I was about eight. My mother left my real father in Walsall when she was pregnant with me and came to Nottingham. I only met my real father once. My mother only deigned to tell me about him when I was about nineteen. I had always assumed that my stepfather was actually my father. To find he's not is a great relief [laughs]. I'd hate to think I was anything genetically connected with him.

My mother came from Kingston, Jamaica. And my stepfather is from St Elizabeth, also in Jamaica. My stepfather arrived here in '57 and my mother probably about the same time. She was not the sort of woman to be tied down. She spent most of her time raving [laughs]. I think I might have inherited that. And I spent most of my time helping her get ready to rave. I helped her to get dressed and took messages round to her boyfriends. My mother had lots of affairs. She just wasn't a one woman, one man person, she says. I wonder if it wasn't just the totally different expectations of society over here. In Jamaica I think she had her first child when she was about thirteen. Contraception doesn't seem to be a word that she ever used. She had eight kids altogether. And that took its toll on her. She couldn't cope.

When my stepfather first came over here he had a job in the ammunitions depot just outside Nottingham, which was where most of the Afro-Caribbeans who came to Nottingham at that time ended up working. He did that for about six or seven years and then he got a job on the buses, and he was there for at least a decade. He was a farmer in Jamaica. Now he works in Boots. That's all I know about him.

When I was very little, I lived in a place called Hyson Green. It was, like, Nottingham's Brixton: bad housing, nothing there, nobody's got jobs. So it was cheap accommodation. We lived there until I was about two or three, then we moved to a terraced house. Two families lived in it and we shared the kitchen and all the facilities. They were nicely kept homes. It was like a typical Jamaican household really. It wasn't a house shared with Trini-dadians or the other Caribbean Island people. There was an element of inbuilt prejudice against all the small island people.

The relationship between my stepfather and mum was bloody horrendous. I really don't know why they ever got married. They just spent all their time arguing, and they were really bad rows; I mean, she would go for him with an *axe*. She was spending all the housekeeping money on raving, and when he was on nights she was off out. I don't think he had a happy time. But then she obviously wasn't happy either. I just don't know why they didn't leave each other a long time before they did.

I was never close to them. I mean they never noticed us. I don't think I liked my mum very much when I was younger. Having said that, I must have done because I was always around her. But she took out on me the fact that her relationship wasn't going well with him. She's always said that I was responsible for the downfall of her life; because I was the first child she had in this country and I was a mistake. I was made into this adult too early, like, mother-ing her. She was brought up in a place where everybody shared looking after their children: that's a traditional thing. And over here she didn't have that. She had her kids and she was expected to look after them.

I remember the first nursery I went to was OK. I looked forward to going, and getting a decent sleep. But I went to about three or four Infants schools. I kept moving on because I had problems drinking milk. I ran away all the time because they made me drink milk. I found it really terrifying. I think that was a result of them not knowing how to deal with Black kids. We were all just starting to go to school then and I just don't think they knew how to handle us. They saw my behaviour as abnormal and they'd attribute it to the fact that I was Black and I was probably suffering from some trauma. I probably was [laughs].

But they didn't take any responsibility on themselves. It was all my or my family's fault.

My brothers and sisters all came more or less one after the other. I've never resented having brothers and sisters. As young kids we all stuck together. There were a lot of us so people didn't mess about with us too much. Sounds really aggressive that, doesn't it? [laughs]

I'm not sure why my mum left. There was no special build up to it. I just remember we came home from school for our lunch and she went off to get us these fish and chips and I'm still waiting for them twenty-odd years later. My father obviously wasn't expecting it because he was in bed, sleeping off nights. I thought something had happened to her. So I went and got him out of bed and he took us back to school. And when we came back she still hadn't come home. He didn't know where she was. That was the last we saw of her until I was seventeen.

After she left, social services got their little claws in [laughs]. My dad was saddled with six kids, but he was quite capable of managing us. He made arrangements for a friend of his to look after us in the day. So he organized that quite well. I don't know why social services were involved. Anyway, next thing I know, the three youngest were taken into foster care and farmed out to some country place where they were the only Black kids and these people didn't have a clue what to do with them. They were just like pets at the zoo I think. My father always tried to get them back.

In the period my mum was around, to be honest, I used to get hit every day practically, for breathing. I knew the inside-out of a Bookies. I had to go and pick her up at the local boozer. Then when she left I suddenly could become a child again. I wouldn't say that I missed her badly, I don't think anybody did. Everybody seemed a lot happier actually. That period of my childhood was the best.

Two years later my father met a white woman through a guy that he worked with. My father is very secretive and he never talked about anything, so I don't know how long the relationship was going on before we actually got to meet her. Anyway, soon we all moved in with this woman, and not long after that, the three youngest were back out of care. It was all done very quickly. I didn't take to it too kindly; I mean we were expected to call this woman 'mother' and I wasn't having that. As it transpired, I got on really well with her and she's done remarkably well. I wouldn't take on somebody else's six bloody kids, especially at that time. It would have been the early sixties and she got a lot of stick because she was a white woman. People said she was 'into Black men'. I don't think she'd had much to do with the Black community before she met my father. I used to get into loads of fights because I wouldn't have anybody putting her down, so on the one hand I did like her, but I just wasn't prepared to call her mum.

By that time I was at Trentbridge Junior School. We had one teacher who taught us until we took our eleven plus, Mr Player. I thought he was wonderful. He had a lot of time for everybody. I did extremely well at school under him. He was quite an old guy, so you'd have thought he would be set in his ways and that teaching the ethnic minorities would have been hard work, but a good 75 per cent of our class got into Grammar School. At the time I met him I'd have been about nine, and I could just about count but not read at all. My stepmother taught me to read and write, and with her and the teacher working hard I passed the eleven plus.

I was meant to go to the Grammar School but I didn't want to because it was the local toff school, so I went to this fucking awful secondary school called Roland Green. I'd say 25 per cent of the kids were Black, and as time went on it became a dumping ground for people expelled from other schools. It was massive as well: one of those new open plan jobs. I got into lots of political arguments with the teachers, although I wouldn't have called them that at the time. They said it was because I was from a mixed marriage. I didn't really know how to deal with them, apart from by just being aggressive, because it was the only way I seemed to get any reaction. The only thing I was successful at in school was athletics. I played most of the sports for the school. I feel bitter about my whole education. People expected us to be able to do sports but not the work. I was there to run or jump and that would get me on in life.

Most of my friends at school were Black girls. Racism was rife. Some teachers were just outright racists: once I helped initiate an all day 'sit-in' because our maths teacher called one of the first-year students 'a monkey'.

When I was about eleven or so my father seemed to completely change. When we were very young we were reasonably close to him because he supplied us with pocket money, and that was quite a big thing because I don't think he could afford it. But when he moved in with my stepmother he started abusing me, and I later discovered that he'd abused all my sisters. It got to the stage where I always tried not to be in the house on my own. I remember when my stepmother went away for a week's holiday: that was the worst week of my life. He used to get me into his room in the day and systematically abuse me. And he used to come into the bathroom: I never had any privacy. I'd have to suss out when he was on shifts, and if he was on lates it was fine because me mum would be there but if he was on earlies that meant mum would still be at work when I came home. Once he tried to get me and I just got the carving knife to him and we were grappling on the floor when one of my sisters came in and saved his life. I was ready to stab him to death. I think he started harassing the other girls at that point, because he used to leave me alone. I wasn't able to tell my stepmother because she wouldn't have believed it: she'd already had two disastrous marriages, anyway.

I wanted to get away from him and I needed a legitimate excuse, so at eighteen I joined the army. Three girls out of four left home because of my stepfather. One of them booked a flight to the States and she actually told my stepmother why. Another sister ended up in a psychiatric hospital for about six months and she tried to kill herself. When I was about twenty I had a big row with my stepfather and this time he kicked me out of the house and said not to come back, and I thought, great. I got a letter from my stepmother six months later saying she wanted me to come home and apologize to me dad. So I rang up and asked her 'Tell me what I'm apologizing for? Dad's spent all these years abusing me and you're expecting me to apologize to him.'

I phoned her again because she was ill in March this year. We couldn't think of anything to say to each other. I was telling her about this interview and she said 'I hope you don't go repeating those things that you've said about your father.' I said, 'You can think what you like and you can choose to believe who you like but I'm not changing what I've said.' I don't know what's happening now because I've not spoken to them since. He's an amazing character. He can sit and read things in the *News of the World* about men abusing their young kids and say things like, 'He

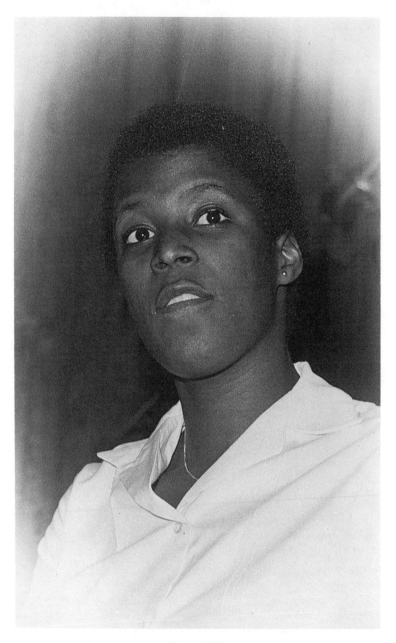

Circa 1977

Women's Royal Army Corps, 1977

should be locked up.' He can't actually see the connection at all. But my adolescent years were hell because of him.

If my stepmother should ever die then I'd really go and challenge him about it, because I think he's got away with it for so long, but it would kill her if I did it now. I couldn't have that on my conscience. It works like that all the time though. You keep it a secret for so long and then it comes out and everybody still thinks you're a liar. The last time I went home, my sister from the States was there. She's got into religion, and forgiven him. It's just one big farce after another. But I'm looking forward to the day when I can make him actually sit down and look at what he's done. I want to reduce him to a wreck.

It definitely affected my schooling. And the memories, God. For a long time I used to have really bad nightmares about it, because even though I was free, it was like he was still haunting me. I was a really miserable kid. My mum's got hundreds of pictures of me at home where I'm never smiling. Nobody ever bothered to find out why.

I met my first lesbian when I was at Secondary School. One of the PE teachers was a lesbian. She got the sack and I was up in arms about that because she was very good at her job. It must have been a real strain for her to be an 'out' lesbian. I thought about being a lesbian from the time I was about fifteen: I told my stepmother when I was about nineteen and she said 'I've suspected that from the time you was about fifteen.' I hated the whole sexual thing with boys. That's not connected to my abuse. Anyway, I fell in love with a student teacher. We are all supposed to go through phases like that but I think at fifteen I knew that's what I wanted out of life. I just didn't know how I was going to go about it.

When I was younger I used to play doctors and nurses – I always used to be the doctor examining the nurses – but my first taste of lesbian sex was when I decided to join the Army. It wasn't all that thrilling either [laughs]. We read the gutter press in our house – *The News of the World* – and at the time there was this big scandal because twenty women had been kicked out of the Army for being lesbians. (*The News of the World* reckoned that if they were to get rid of them all there'd be nobody in the WRAC.) I thought 'Oh, this is my chance to find out what it's all about.' I did six weeks training at Guildford and then we went to Mill Hill in London. I got this mad crush on this woman and she introduced me to clubs and places like Gateways. Now I look back on it I think, God, they were really seedy and horrible, but I had to start somewhere. I was madly in love with this woman but nothing ever came of it. Then my two best-friends wanted to know where I was going at weekends. So I told them and they came out with me one night, and it turned out one of the girls had a crush on me. So we had this sort of fling. It wasn't anything heavy. We really weren't sure what we were doing. That was my first affair.

I hated most of the women in the army. It was just like they'd recruited morons and I wondered how I'd got in. Training involved getting up really early in the morning [laughs] and being awake at midnight pressing your clothes. We did things like map reading, which I was absolutely useless at, and the first aid was almost as bad in that I can't stand blood. But I enjoyed the training because we were all in the same boat and the people who were in charge were so silly. I was in the same platoon as the only other Black woman. I think they put us together to keep each other company. After training for six weeks you have this fantastic passing out parade where your parents come along and say 'Oh look at our Milly, hasn't she done wonderfully well? Doesn't she look nice in that uniform?'

After training I went to Ireland for about eighteen months. I didn't know anything about Ireland and the army don't tell you anything except that the IRA are the bad guys and the Protestants are the good guys. I worked as a clerk in the intelligence section, collating information. Somebody would say 'I want a file on Gerry Adams' so I'd get twenty on him which told you everything from the colour of his socks to the last time he went to the toilet.

I was very lucky not to have been investigated as a lesbian in the army. It's against military law to be a lesbian although if they looked at it logically they would realize that the people who stay in the Army longest are those that are not going to get married. They make it a career, and nine times out of ten they're lesbians. I only ever had one incident, when the Military Police raided all the rooms and everyone was leaping out of windows. The army know all along who is and who isn't. It still goes on; there's a big investigation on now. I've never actually experienced the humiliation but women have said they've been dragged out of bed at four o'clock in the morning and all they've had on is their nightie or bra and knickers and they're kept in a cold room for hours on end and had some really disgusting remarks made to them.

In the army lesbians were either butch or femme, but if you were like me you were nothing in particular and people didn't know what to make of you. A lot of lesbians drank too much. They earned a lot of money and they spent it on drink. And the other thing was the racism in the Army, which goes right from the top to the bottom. I didn't like any of those women anyway but it would never have entered their head to have a relationship with a Black woman. Most of the Black women that were there were straight so the few that weren't had to stick together.

The first serious relationship I had lasted about eight months, but it ended really nastily, particularly because of racism. If I've spent a long time with somebody and then they turn round and say something that's really racist, I just flip my lid. For six months after we split up I kept myself to myself, and I was a lot better for it as well.

The army started talking about getting the women to learn how to use guns. When I signed up there was nothing there that said I had to do that. They said it would affect my career but I told them it wouldn't because I was leaving. So I just put my notice in. I had a terrible last eighteen months.

I got sent to Aldershot where there was this woman who basically hated Black people. I was on valium because I couldn't cope with all the crap anymore. I was also an NCO so I was in a position of responsibility, and I had a conflict of interests because my loyalties were supposed to be with my superiors but my real loyalty was to the women I was supposed to be organizing. Leaving the army was the best decision of my life and I did it with style. When you leave the army there is a whole series of things you have to do; medical and dental check-up, kit inspection, and it all goes on for weeks and on the day you leave you have to hand in your ID card, sign the Official Secrets Act and another form to say you won't visit any communist countries for three years. Then you have to go to the commanding officer to have your farewell interviews. I went and handed in my ID card but I refused to sign any of the papers and I told the commanding officer that I had nothing to say to her. This was unheard of, as people always follow the letter of the law when they leave, but I just wanted to find a way to say 'up yours'.

After I left I stayed in Guildford for about six months but I couldn't get a job on the cards and I had two really bad racist attacks while I was there. So I was ready for a change when I met this woman from Brighton at a party and I decided to move there myself. Soon after I got there the relationship fell through. That made me feel like giving up, but not long after that I met up with an Irish Catholic woman and that was the start of the turning point of my life.

On our first date we sat in the park and I thought I'd better tell this woman I've been in the Army because she isn't going to like it a lot. So we spent hours and hours talking about Ireland and she told me a lot that I hadn't realized. From that the relationship developed. I wasn't ever really clear that I loved her but I felt quite safe with her and she's a really nice person, but there were lots of things about us that were just not compatible. Because this woman was an Irish Catholic, I wasn't allowed to have any of my friends from the Army come to visit the house – which was understandable – but it got a bit much when I used the car to go and see them once and she just went loopy. We used to have constant arguments because I felt quite isolated and I didn't like any of her friends. In the end I just said I wanted to call it a day and we are still trying to build up some sort of friendship.

I never really thought about politics and I'm not a great political person now, but because of the relationship I began to come in contact with feminism. My first social gathering with a bunch of feminists was a beach party. They were all sitting there listening to some women howling on this cassette. (Fortunately they said bring some music, so I brought a Grace Jones tape which was about as tactful as I could possibly get.) Anyway, they all sat there in duffle coats and round specs and with cropped hair professing to be working-class women who were being constantly harassed. But they all had some sort of University background and I just thought, 'What do they know about my lifestyle?'

Since then I've been more involved with feminism. I still can't be bothered with all these women who spend their time preaching hatred about men. We can't get rid of men. A lot of the feminists I met initially were middle-class white women. Feminism did give me an awareness of a political language though. In the army I was a non-conformist and feminism gave me a way of understanding that, even though a lot of it was over the top.

179

It was at this time that I got a job working at a girls' hostel in London. There were two other Black women there, so I felt supported for the first time in years of employment. Alice was a strong Black woman who'd been around Black people all her life and knew exactly where she was going. (I suppose Alice would disagree with that but I always thought she knew exactly where she was going.) Bernice had been brought up in a white area in Stevenage so we had more similarities because I'd spent all my time among white people. The three of us learnt a lot from each other and working with young women gave me scope to test my own arguments and theories.

While I was there, two women came from the Incest Survivors Campaign to talk to the staff group. Afterwards the head of the home stood up and said, 'We can't understand because we haven't been there ourselves.' And from that time on I never got on with her, because she hadn't ever considered that any of the misfortunes that have happened to young people in care also might have happened to us. Subsequently two of us went to this course where there was a woman from the Child Sexual Abuse project. The thing that really shocked me was that the woman who led the course had taken into account that she was talking to women who might have been through all of it.

The way I've dealt with my incest is by talking to people in the same situation. At the Black Lesbian Conference I felt safe enough for the first time to speak about it in a group. I've spent a lot of years pretending it was a thing in the past, but actually it has always been eating away at me.

One of the things that has come up is the issue of guilt. Now, if anybody ever said to me 'What were you like when you were younger?' I would say I was a 'promiscuous' little girl who was searching for something – god knows what – and in the end I got abused by lots of people, not just my father. People can say that was my choice, but I don't think there was any choice. As a child that's the only way I saw of getting any attention.

After the hostel work I got a job in Tower Hamlets in the fostering and adoption team. When I read through a lot of their case histories I couldn't *believe* them. Because they're from those backgrounds themselves they had a whole policy of fostering Black kids off to middle-class white families for experimentation purposes. There was one case where a young, mixed race boy was fostered off to a family with six other Black kids, and the husband was a psychiatrist who was writing a book. Now I've read extracts from this book and as far as I'm concerned he used those kids as guinea pigs. I left because I just didn't have any time for the bureaucracy.

Now I work for a housing association that caters for young lesbians and gays, which is a welcome relief. Being a lesbian is an ordinary thing in that atmosphere. It's not realistic at times because once you've dealt with all these different lesbian and gay organizations you tend to go home at night and think everybody on the tube's looking at you. When I was leaving Tower Hamlets I had to look at my choices about what I wanted to do and I decided to go back to college. The options really for me were social work, teaching or law. I chose law. Part of the reason is because of the big class barrier. I feel quite strongly, having looked at various law syllabuses, that I don't think it's beyond the grasp of an ordinary working class person. I want to do a law course partly because I feel like I'm going to die without having achieved anything. I also want to prove something to my parents, because they just assume that we've all been great failures. I have to leave Stonewall which I don't like doing, but after all, if Maggie Thatcher gets in again I'll need a good qualification so I can leave the country.

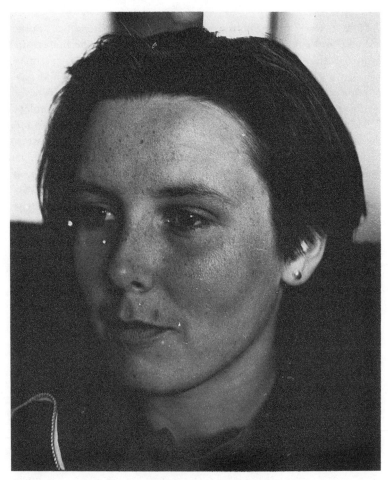

Portrait of Lynne Connolly

LYNNE CONNOLLY

INTERVIEWED ON 21 DECEMBER 1987 BY
ALLEGRA DAMJI

I was born in East Belfast in 1962. My mum was in hospital shortly after. I found out a few years ago that that was because she had a nervous breakdown and was in a psychiatric unit. I've got four brothers. We were supposed to be looked after by my father but, basically, he didn't want responsibility for the children, so I was taken care of by two women who were neighbours and friends of my mum. One of them had a little girl. She had been married and then decided she had had enough and left to set up home with this other woman. And they are still together, after thirty years or so.

I have a lot of childhood memories of them. The little girl had a stuffed dog with wheels and I used to play on it all the time. It was brilliant [laughs]. I always knew they were living together but they were just friendly aunty figures to me. Just thinking back I realized there was something going on there. It was very unusual in Belfast to meet women, unless they were related, living together for so long. A few years ago I was talking about them to my mum and she said, did I know they were gay?

My father had loads of different jobs, from milkman to pools agent. Nothing exciting [laughs]. They didn't bring in much money and my mum didn't work while she was looking after us. When I was very young I remember being with my mum a lot. My father was always out and about. His parents still lived in Belfast and I saw them once a week. My granny used to do mass baking for us all and bring candy apples. My mum's whole family moved to England when she got married at sixteen. She was the

183

only one left out of ten children and she lost all that contact at one go. I was always close to my mum, especially because I was the only girl.

I remember enjoying primary school. I got on well with people and I was quite good at English and writing stories. We moved a lot and each time it was to a better place. We were the 'roughs' moving in: you could pick that up from people. With five kids altogether we were quite a rowdy family and there was always complaints about everything. My mum couldn't often afford to buy me any decent clothes or anything that was fashionable. Most of our clothes were sent over by the relations in England. I got quite a few comments about what I was wearing and that was awful. I used to say, 'If you don't like it, that's tough shit really. Because I haven't got anything else' [laughs]. But we were definitely getting bigger houses and my dad was always getting new cars. Both my parents were from poor families. My dad definitely wanted a house and a car: male possessions! My mum wanted more comfort for her and the kids. I suppose what I'm saying is my dad's interests were more selfish rather than family orientated.

We were Protestants but I didn't really think about it when I was growing up. I guess I didn't have to, but I could never understand the idea that you hated someone just because they happen to be Catholic.

My dad always drank a lot. One night I was found by the neighbours screaming my eyes out because I had something wrong with my ears. I was really wee and my dad was meant to be there but he was out drinking. Things like that have been told to me afterwards. When we were quite young we were always in bed when he came back drunk but as I got older I started realizing things. I used to wake up and hear my mum crying because she was getting hit. It was me who noticed it. My brothers were always out for the count. At first I didn't really understand it. That was when I was about nine or ten. Then I started going to the bedroom to see what was going on but I just got turfed out again. I started being abusive to my dad as well. I just thought, 'Who does he think he is? And if he can behave like that to other people, I can say anything I want to him.' So if he said I was talking a load of shit I would start answering back saying 'The only person I know around here who talks shit is you.' He'd slap me in the face. I just completely lost all respect for him.

Because I was so close to my mum I did pick up more. My brothers didn't notice anything. A year or two ago one of them said how he couldn't understand why I didn't like my dad. He didn't know half of what had been going on. In fact they all think I'm a bit over the top about my dad. It was a lot to do with me and my mum, we were really close: a bit too close in a lot of ways. She started telling me things me dad was doing and how he treated her, and it was too much for me to cope with. I didn't really need to know all that, but she didn't have anyone else to talk to, and I wanted to comfort her. We'd lie there and hear the car coming up the driveway and all the lights would be out and I would just creep across the floor into my bedroom. That happened most nights. Sometimes we used to sneak out and get Chinese take-aways and eat them at night time and nobody else got any.

My brothers recognized that my mum and I had a special relationship. At times I think they felt a bit funny about that. There was a while that my mum slept with me because she didn't want to sleep with me dad anymore. I had this wee single bed and I remember we used to hug each other really tight every night before going to sleep and just feeling her against me. One night in particular he come home really drunk and grabbed my mum by the hair and trailed her out of my bed and told her to get into their bed because she was his wife and was meant to be in the bedroom. I jumped up and tried to push him off because he was really thumping her. He just threw me across the room and one of my brothers came in and head-butted him and knocked him out, which was brilliant. When my dad came to, he went downstairs and was rattling through the cutlery, and we thought he was going to come with a knife and stab us all. It was really terrifying. After that my ma said she was definitely going to get a separation, because now the children had become involved. For the month it took for the lawyers to sort out the separation it was desperate living at home. There were just terrible fights and everyone was involved.

My mum had left three or four times throughout the marriage. There was a couple of times that we all went to talk with my granny Connolly and then we went over to my mum's relations in England. She must have saved up for ages for it. My dad, when he found out where we were, was phoning and saying he loved and missed us. I never believed him. I could have quite happily done without him. But my mum had a bit of a notion of standing by her husband, and she must have believed him when he said he would give up drink and things would change. She also had five children to look after with no money so we came back.

I started losing interest in school because of what was happening at home. I went to a big Comprehensive girls' school. I thought I should have passed my eleven plus. School to me was just mucking about with my mates, mitching off and eating biscuits all day. I started getting really introverted and closed off. One teacher in particular noticed there was something wrong and she used to take me into the storeroom and give me hugs every day. I used to stand there trying to be dead insolent: like, 'What the fuck are you doing this for?' But I quite enjoyed feeling her press her breasts into my face [laughs]. It happened for a couple of years. I'm surprised she didn't get the sack.

Some of my early sexual memories were with my brothers. This was when I was about eleven and my brother was thirteen. We were both developing a bit and it was like real interest and intrigue. We used to play about. He showed me how he masturbated and I jerked him off and he touched me a lot with his fingers. I also used to experiment with my younger brother. He probably hates me now you know [laughs]. But this friend and I used to experiment with him. He was the patient and we were the doctors. I used to make him take his pants down and lay on the bed and we would poke him and play with him [laughs] and then send him out and we'd play with each other. My wee brother told my mum once. I just said he was making it up because he didn't like me [laughs]. Probably scarred him for life. My friend was a couple of years older than me so she was more developed and that was really exciting. There was this one day I was sitting in the front-room with her in the afternoon and we had the curtains pulled down and I was on her knee with my hand up her jumper on her breasts and my ma walked in and said 'What are you doing?' I said we were playing houses or something [laughs]. And she just pulled the curtains open and said, 'Oh well, don't pull the curtains in the daytime.' I thought I was for it.

Another vivid memory is my father's car. He had one that was new and sporty, and it was his pride and joy. He wouldn't let us kids near it but the boys loved it. Anyway, one night I was in bed and I heard what I thought was thunder and lightning and there was this red glow at the window. So I looked out and this little pride and joy was on fire. So I sort of tiptoed in the bedroom and I says 'The car's on fire'. He flew out of bed and he had no clothes on and I didn't know whether to laugh or look at the wall. My brothers eventually got up and they're going, 'Oh my God, it's awful', and I muttered, 'Serves him right', and my mum cuffed my ear. I remember standing there watching it go up in flames and feeling sort of happy. He was involved in some shady deals and had enemies. Somebody had set it on fire and it had no insurance either [laughs].

I didn't talk to anybody about what was going on at home. I just thought 'Who's going to believe me?', and that it was all so emotional and upsetting that I didn't know where to start. I thought I had to look after my mum, basically. I was not really thinking about what I was going through at all. After I left school I took an overdose because I couldn't cope and wanted a way out. I remember phoning one of the teachers up and she came and took me to hospital. I took another a couple of days later. I remember people standing around and saying, 'You wonder why they do it, especially twice in a week.' I was just this lump of meat. They did recommend help though, and I went to a psychiatric unit for about a month. A psychologist bloke there tried to get me to have more confidence in myself. I thought I was really thick because my dad was always telling me I was. He did that to everyone in the family.

I did O levels and passed three, and when I left school I started working as a nursing assistant at this private nursing home. It was hardly any money and shit work, so I didn't stay long. I felt for a couple of years my sexuality had been ignored because I was so distracted by things at home, so when things had eased down I started thinking about my sexuality a bit more, and it was easier to get off with blokes. So, I did that for a bit, but I never really enjoyed it. Most blokes were pretty ignorant about how to have sex that was enjoyable for a woman. That was my main impression. I always knew that I identified a lot more strongly with women; I'm sure it's a lot to do with having such a close relationship with my mum. It was nice being that close to a woman, and physically and sexually I was interested in women's bodies.

Religion was a real pressure, though. People think of religion

Family holiday, Ireland, 1963

Lynne with brother, circa 1975

188

in Ireland as the Catholic Church, but I went to a Baptist Church and they were just head cases. It was hard to stop thinking that I was going to hell and that my life was a complete waste. But I thought there was no point in trying to be something that wasn't me.

When I was eighteen I moved to Sunderland for a couple of months. Basically I wanted to get away from Belfast and family life. It just felt like a huge cloud over me that I couldn't get rid of. I definitely wanted to get off with a woman as well. I just thought it would be easier to do if I was away from my home town and without the family pressure. I met somebody who knew somebody who was prepared to let me stay for a while. When I got there I got in touch with the Women's Centre, and I met this woman. I just decided I wanted to sleep with her because I wanted to sleep with a woman, so I did. It was good and I was glad that I'd got around to doing it because I knew that was what I wanted. For ages I'd been saying that I was bisexual because I definitely knew I wasn't dead straight, but now I felt quite clear and I stayed a few months and went back to Belfast to a flat on my own.

I told a few friends that I'd been at school with and some of them really freaked out about it. I remember once playing this record – I think it was *The Lesbian Concentrate* [laughs] – at a friend's house and she was really shocked and said 'Don't bring political records in the house again, my father doesn't like them.' But I was quite happy to tell people I was a lesbian. I knew it would annoy and shock some people and I wanted to do that. Another friend completely dropped me. It was quite funny because she went through this bit of saying, 'Of course, I'm not going to be funny about touching you just because you're a lesbian.' She used to be a very warm, cuddly sort of person, and we used to hug all the time. One night she came round for a drink and we were just sitting there and she put her arm round me, to prove a point, but she was completely rigid. I gave up on her because she reacted so badly. Then I tried to get in touch with lesbians in Belfast through Lesbian Line. I was in for a bit of a shock [laughs]. It was dead 'butch and femme' and, because it was a small town, fairly incestuous. It was little groups of people who didn't speak to each other for various reasons. Someone would always be over saying, 'Don't you speak to them because they're like this, you know.' I was bombarded with all this and I thought,

189

'But who the hell *am* I meant to speak to?' I decided to ignore all that and find out for myself. I was a new face on the scene and people were dying for new blood [laughs]. It felt like that, and then it was like the butch thing about 'What side do you think I should wear my keys on?' and I thought, I don't know, what does it all mean? I didn't want anything to do with it after a while, so I gave it a miss for nearly a year.

I started buying *Spare Rib*, because I thought there might be some juicy bits about lesbians in there, but there wasn't a lot of that. I read *The Well of Loneliness*, but there wasn't a lot of excitement there either, so I used to write stuff myself about fantasies to do with women. I used to order *Spare Rib* from the local shop and they used to read it before I got it and ask me questions about it. My neighbours didn't quite know what to make of me. In fact one of them thought I was running a brothel! [laughs]

It was when I moved to another house that I said a woman who was having trouble with her parents could move in with me. A friend of hers kept coming to visit. She was about seventeen and still at school and we were attracted to each other. The woman I had staying turned out to be a pain in the arse, so I had to get her to leave. Judith was helping her move out and just as she was going I said something like, 'You don't have to stop visiting just because thingy's left', and she says, 'No, I didn't intend to.' So we went from there and she started calling round and we got off with each other.

It was very up and down. There was a lot of pressure from her parents, who hated me because I was working class. They wanted her to do well in her A levels and thought I was a bad influence because I was older and on the dole. They tried to stop any contact. Obviously she rebelled against that and came to visit me all the time when she should have been studying. At that time I was trying to sort out what I wanted to do with myself as well. I was doing A levels through a correspondence course and planning to move to London, so there was a lot of unsettling things. But sexually it was good fun because it was the first time she had slept with anyone and it was my first involved relationship, and we did care for each other a lot. It ended just before I moved to London. She was getting worn down by her parents and started saying things about us not getting on because of the difference in class. I felt she was too dependent on me. So that was a bit messy.

I don't think it was handled very well by either of us, but you don't have anything to go by the first time you finish with someone.

I wanted to do social work when I'd passed my A levels. I wanted to help people because I'd had a hard time myself, but I kept changing my mind and I ended up applying to Middlesex Poly to do a sociology degree. So I moved to London and I did the first year of the course, but I found it really dry and boring. Just before I left Belfast somebody had showed me how to develop film and do photographic prints, and I really got into that. I spent most of my first year at Middlesex using their darkroom and all their materials, and then I applied to do a photography degree at Central London Poly. When I applied the course was full so I had to wait a year. They were a bit concerned that I wouldn't be able to do the theory – a lot about psychoanalysis and how it relates to imagery – so I had to write an essay for them, but that was okay. I liked photography because it meant doing something physical and using technical equipment to produce something creative. For me it is important to do work with some political or social meaning, and photography can do that if you want it to.

I was also trying to see what was going on in the lesbian scene in London. I came out to people at Middlesex Poly when I was there and they were quite shocked because they had just left school and were dead straight. Then I started meeting lesbians. I was scared because London was so big and I wasn't sure how different the scene would be here, but I met this woman called Cath and I ended up going out with her for about two and a half years, and I lived with her for about a year of that. That was a lot to do with my settling in London. We met when we were both working in the printing trade and I thought she was dead friendly. She talked a lot and I don't very much, so it really annoys me sometimes when people do, but I liked the fact she did, for some reason. I still felt funny about being new to London. It was just nice to sit there and let somebody rabbit on, but after a while it drove me mad [laughs].

One of my brothers came to stay when I was living with Cath and I got really fed up having to be discreet, so I just told him I was a lesbian and he had to like it or lump it. He said he knew anyway, and then I told my sister-in-law because I got on really well with her. It was beyond anything that related to her life, but

191

she was really good and said, 'Well, at least I'll know not to go on about boyfriends and you must be fed up listening to me.' Then she said that she thought my dad knew somehow. That made me want to tell my mum because I didn't want him telling her and using it to be spiteful, so I wrote and told her a couple of years ago. She didn't contact me for a while so I phoned her up. I was crying down the phone and she was saying, 'Don't worry about it, I still love you, you're still my daughter.' Two days later she phoned and she was really angry and saying I was going to hell. I think it had just hit her, but then she also said about six months before that she had a dream where I was a lesbian [laughs]. So I think she did know for a while but just didn't want to admit it. We just talked a lot and she thought it was a perversion and unnatural, and I'd never be happy and lead a normal life, and I wouldn't be able to have babies. I didn't tell her that I could have babies if I wanted, I think that would have been more upsetting [laughs].

So far, most of my brothers and my mum have met people I've been having relationships with. Generally I think they've tried to be friendly but can't get to grips with it. Cath came over with me a few years ago and it was awkward, mostly because I was bringing part of my life in London, and my relationship, back to my home and family. They couldn't handle it and neither could I, so it wasn't such a good combination. Cath and I split up just over two years ago but remain very close friends.

More recently, things seem to have improved a lot with some of my family, especially my mum. The last time I was home was with Sarah – the woman I'm involved with now – last summer, and my mum was really friendly and welcoming. It was great! That trip home was significant in lots of ways. It's important for me to be able to go home with lovers as a lot of my life and background isn't represented by life in London. Further, it's especially important that my family do accept me being lesbian and consequently accept my lovers. Also, returning from Belfast that time I met up with Judith who I hadn't seen for years, and it's been good to pick up contact with her again.

Things seem to have really progressed in many ways: I'm now finishing the photography degree, which feels like a huge achievement (including facing the problems inherent in a middle-class education system) and am involved in a *Copy Art Against the Clause* exhibition. I've also just got a new motorbike which is very nice, and my dog's just got over a phantom pregnancy, and life goes on.

Balham, London, 1986. Portrait by Nicky West

LIZ NAYLOR

INTERVIEWED ON 11 MARCH 1986 BY
MARGOT FARNHAM

I was born in Nuneaton, in Warwickshire, in September 1962. I never knew my father because he died when I was three, but both him and my mother came from working-class Liverpool backgrounds. My father was a school teacher. During the war, my mother drove round the country for a firm that sold urns to farmers, and I think that was the happiest time of her life. But it was the usual story and then the men came back.

My sister is seven years older than me. When I was born, my parents had just bought a new house and everything was looking as if they would be set for a life of domestic comfort. But this totally changed when my father died. My mother just never recovered from it: she went into this massive grief. She had to work and she wasn't trained, which meant that we were poor.

When my father died, my grandmother moved in to our house. My grandmother used to make us eat mutton and I remember being naughty and her smacking us. My Aunty Barbara was the younger daughter and I remember her being like a big sister. I really liked her and she kind of looked after me as my mother was at work. And then we moved up to Liverpool when I was about five. I think my mother just wanted to get away from the memories of my father. In Liverpool she became very ill with anaemia and didn't work, and I can remember just starting school and her always being in her bedroom, ill. We didn't really stay there very long, but I have very fond memories of the sea at New Brighton and Wallasey.

We had lived in a place called Tamworth in the Midlands and

Liverpool seemed really huge, and I remember my first day at school clearly. It was the first time I'd ever worn a skirt, a little tartan skirt. I remember going to the toilet and pulling this skirt down because it never occurred to me that you could lift skirts up. I just cried. I hated it. And they taught phonetic reading. I felt really out of place but it was by the sea – well the Mersey – which I loved. Spring tides used to come and rip up the prom front and we used to throw things at jellyfish on the beach. Those early memories seem to revolve around playing out all the time, and we didn't have a home like kids seem to have homes. My mother was rather distant and not there and we just played out all the time. I had a best-friend, a boy. I thought boys were much more exciting than girls and I remember having a complete set of Matchbox cars in a little carrying case.

In Liverpool it was my sister who looked after me when she got back from school. We were always close as little kids. She was into football and she used to make little magazines for me. The biggest memory of my mother, very early on, is just her not being there. She was still very emotionally wrapped up in her own grief.

When I was six we moved from Liverpool to the village of Austrey where my father and mother first lived when they were married. It had one shop and one bus into Tamworth, which is about seven miles away. I started at a village school which had three teachers and was just one room. We rented a tied cottage with an acre and a half of wilderness. It had a damson tree and two apple trees and a well, and it was brilliant. We lived there from when I was about six till I was about eight. I was absolutely in my element. I didn't have to wear skirts. At school I had to be taught to read and our cottage was next door to the school, but it was not like school. I spent most of my time building dens, which was my other great passion. My grandmother had moved into the village too. She lived down the other end of the village.

When my mother had recovered from her anaemia she got a job in Tamworth as a secretary, and my grandmother used to get my tea and things, but all that I remember is being out all the time again, building dens. It's amazing how absorbing climbing a tree can be. My sister was going to secondary school now, and she had a suedehead boyfriend with a Crombie. Inevitably it would be like, 'Go home; don't follow us', but most of the time it was pretty OK so I was always in quite adult company it seems. I was just incredibly happy, totally carefree and in this spooky old cottage. It was just rambling. It had beams and a big fire, but it wasn't done up and it was called The Old Cottage. There was loads of land around, little spinneys and tyres for swings. I remember books like *Ned the Lonely Donkey*, but we weren't encouraged to read. My sister used to get *Shoot* and *Goal* every week and I read football comics. I remember begging my mother to buy me a pair of Tuf boys slip-on shoes with elasticated sides, and she eventually relented and she also bought me a little denim jacket, which I was incredibly proud of and I always wore jeans with elasticated waists from Woolies and I wanted to be a boy.

I found a penknife in the fields and I was really proud of it and I just thought, 'Show a penknife to a girl and they're not interested, but boys are like "Wow! She's got a penknife!"' I also found boys quite easy to manipulate. They always seemed to be quite impressed by my freedom as I didn't have to be in at certain times and I was tough.

At nine we moved to the market town of Tamworth again. My mother's boss decided to buy a corner shop and my mother looked after it. I had to move to another big Victorian horrible-corridored school, which I hated. That's when I started not going to school. After this little village school, I was suddenly just another new kid. I never made friends there at all and also, at that age, going on for nine, it seems like education starts to be hard. Tamworth has a big castle tower in grounds and I used to just go and play in the grounds. At night I played football almost constantly in the street with a gang of a lot older boys and this was when I started to become, I think, troublesome to my mother. I was a happy blissed-out kid building dens before, but then I started to smoke. I also used to be in fights and sometimes come back with a bleeding mouth and it's the first time I can remember my mother saying, 'You can't do these things.' It's the first time I remember her being concerned. I used to truant and I remember the Truant Officer coming to the shop. My sister was doing her O levels. She had suddenly become very serious and scholarly.

I think my mother was very unhappy running this shop; I just don't think she's ever settled down and we didn't have that much money, but up North houses are quite cheap and we got this terraced house in an Asian street. Midlands towns are all rather bland, I think, and suddenly it was really 'Up-North L.S. Lowry'.

I spent about a year at the Primary School which is opposite and I quite liked that. It was filled with Asian kids. I was a big noise again, and my mother got a job as a secretary in the psychiatric unit of all places and I got my own key to the house.

At this primary school I was taught by this guy, Peter Walker; he had quite long hair and little round John Lennon glasses and English was his specialist subject. He was really friendly and I immediately stuck out as I still used to wear jeans. He just latched onto me and he said 'Have this record'. It was by Captain Beefheart and I took it home and listened to it. Because I liked him so much I started to take an interest in writing. It was the first time I really started intellectually discovering things and I wanted to know about drugs and I started writing for myself, poetry; a lot of it was like re-hashing Dylan songs, very much in imitation of the music I was listening to. I wanted that culture so much. I used to make little books and bind them with sellotape. I destroyed them, but I wish now that I'd kept them because they were like books of a ten, going on eleven-year-old who wanted an underground culture. I eventually badgered my mother to buy me an acoustic guitar which I couldn't play at all. I had no musical ability whatsoever.

I was not interested at all in boys as sexual encounters. I didn't know that I was gay particularly; I just cut off all those feelings. But I passed the eleven plus and my mother decided in her great wisdom, because she's a snob, that I should go to Astley Grammar for Girls in Hyde which was about five miles away, as it had a good reputation. It was a State school but it was dead snobby. You had to wear a bottle-green skirt, a green and white blouse and a green cardigan. No tie unfortunately. I arrived, a fat eleven-year-old; I'd tried to grow my hair to a Janis Joplin style during the summer and my mother had got me this second-hand brief-case. I just remember turning up on the first day and it was full of pony-riding doctors' daughters who were into playing at being ballerinas, and I was suddenly thrown into my worst nightmare. Not only was I again a new kid in town but I didn't have a new Parker pen. They were just dead flash and all from self-made Northern businessmen-type families and I think from the very first day I realized that it was going to be bloody awful.

I was into being a hippy and they singled me out as a freak and I used that as a kind of aloofness of 'I am better than you. I have my big adult friend, Peter Walker, and I talk with adults and I read this and I listen to this.' Prior to that I was quite happy trundling on, writing my poems but then all these little girls were into gymnastics and that made me feel very awkward and freaky. I remember from my briefcase to my body, I felt shoddy.

By the second and third year I just used to get a bus and go into Manchester. I started to realize that I was a lesbian but I could never say the word, not even to myself in the bedroom. I'd see these 50-year-old women at school, and one was tall and thin, a Geography teacher, and one was squat, a Maths teacher, and I saw that as lesbian and thought, 'Oh God'. I started to be aware of sexual feelings for the first time and it also suddenly dawned on me that I just didn't like boys. But I think a lot of my confusion over my sexuality came because I saw these horrible lesbians around and also I felt no attraction to girls of my age. My great role model was Janis Joplin.

In the third year, an English teacher called Mrs Davis gave me J.D. Salinger, *Catcher in the Rye*, and that was it, I was Holden Caulfield. It's such a corny book and it must have happened for millions of people. This English teacher gave it to me on my own and it made me feel special. It was a book about an adolescent that was too grown up and it was exactly how I felt. I used to come home and take my school uniform off. I had a pair of flared denims with a different coloured V in and was very proud of them, and I used to go into Manchester to Grass Roots bookshop and started reading a magazine called *Mole Express* which was an alternative underground magazine.

In the third year I tried to buckle down after a visit from the Truancy Officer. My sister had moved up by that time and was attending the local college, doing an art course, and we used to listen to rock records and kept scrap books. My father's sister died of cancer and she gave us some money so my mother sold the terrible terraced house and we moved to Gee Cross. You're doing well if you've moved to Gee Cross and my mother was really delighted to have got away from Scruffy Street. And then in the fourth year I had an English teacher, Elizabeth Levis. And that was the most phenomenal year of my life.

I was this freaky kind of miserable child and we just clicked, and my friendship with her got me through that fourth year. It sounds melodramatic but I think she really did save my life. She got me to write stories and at lunch times we talked and she gave me James Joyce. I was in love with her and all I did at night was sit in my room, writing stream of consciousness, much inspired by James Joyce [laughs]. All I remember about my fourth year was this consuming affair I had with my English teacher: and I wouldn't have her in the fifth year! At the end of that year I think I knew that it had gone too far; I was so far off centre that I couldn't fit in anymore. I was also getting reasonably politicized from the underground literature I was reading. I hated where we lived because it was like Snob Street. Before, I had this blind fury, but when I was fifteen I started to think, 'I hate it because of all it stands for.' I started to understand about my sexuality a little more and at the end of the fourth year I'd almost made up my mind that I couldn't go back there, but more of which later [laughs].

Another important thing was that every summer from when I was about eleven, I went on holiday in the Lake District with my aunty Barbara and her illegitimate child. She chose to have a child and bring it up. I discovered that I liked the countryside and my aunty Barbara talked to me like an adult. She was really great, and it sounds silly, but she smoked and my mother is non-smoking and hardly drinks, so to be with somebody who was relaxed enough to smoke and have the odd drink was very good for me. I was much closer to her than my mother. We used to find really obscure spots; I loved the quietness and it was beautiful.

During that summer after the fourth year, I was fifteen and punk was about to happen. I wasn't involved yet; it was all in London and I didn't go to gigs but I was getting whiffs of that. I did go to a concert at Droylsden Hall. It was a band called The Distractions who were a bit pre-punk, played quite fast music. I went on my own, and the bass player came up to talk to me and I thought, 'Oh God, it's a boy', but it was a girl called Pip who was the first lesbian that I'd ever met and I was overjoyed. My mother picked me up and I said, 'Oh, I've met this girl called Pip and she came up and talked to me', and my mother said, 'I hope she's not a lesbian' and in my heart I was kind of going, 'Yes!' [laughs] but I said, 'Oh no, I don't think so.'

Pip took me to my first gay pub, the Union Tavern, and the Manchester gay scene was just incredible. I walked into the Union. I was always quite short. I felt, 'Oh God, I'm not going to get served, this is going to be really embarrassing.' I'd never really been in a pub before. I walked in and I was really nervous: it was like a Hogarth print. It was mainly a prostitute pub. You know, it was like everybody totally freaky went there. Lots of transvestites, with six-foot-tall bouffants and it was just wild. Drugs were openly being sold [laughs] and I couldn't believe it; it was my chance to take drugs, they were openly being smoked. I got served, no trouble. They knew I was under-aged but it didn't really matter, did it. Pip took me to the table of her lesbian friends who were all prostitutes; they were gay girls, they didn't call themselves lesbians. They were being beaten up by men and they decided they would have affairs with each other. I would sit at the table with them not saying a word. After I'd been in once with Pip I could go in on my own and I used to stay away quite late on Friday nights and my mum worried about me. I'd bought my first three-for-a-pound blue pills and tried my first dope which made me feel very ill [laughs]. I started drinking for the first time, too.

There was a Distractions gig at Hyde Town Hall. Pip introduced me to this woman who at the end of the evening said, 'I'm going to take you home' and I went, 'Oh' [laughs]. She didn't make any obvious overtures. Just at the end of the evening we got in a taxi and it drove to Mossley, which was like a hippy place with lots of cheap mill housing. It was an incredible house. Two up, two down. No electricity in her bedroom. I was terrified. I was just rigid and I took some coaxing into bed and she managed to prise my clothes off and by this time I'd sobered up rapidly [laughs]; she was feeling really wasted because she was on a speed come-down and I said, 'Oh I've never slept with anybody before' and she was like 'Oh shit, what have I picked up?' So she thought, 'Oh well try and get some sleep.' Going on for dawn, a stone was thrown at the window and she let in a very drunken, bearded Scottish man with a bottle of whisky. We woke up the next morning and it was one of those awful situations where you think, 'Oh god, I wish I wasn't here' [laughs]. She was quite kind to me really; I'd told her, 'I live at home with my mother and I go to the Girls' Grammar School.' And I got the bus and went home.

My mum was furious, really sick with worry and asked me where I'd been and I said I'd stayed at friends of Pips. I looked

Held by sister, aged 1

Circa aged 16

Circa aged 16

Glass Animals (also known as The Gay Animals)

203

pretty awful too. About a day later I went to see Pip and I told her about it and I found out that this woman had gonorrhoea and people said, 'Oh no, what did you do?' I was really worried. I didn't really understand such things. But I'd slept with a woman and the summer went on like that. Punk happened bigger, I had my hair cut short and me ear pierced and wore pyjamas, and I was the first punk rocker in Hyde. You know, punk rockers! I bought The Fall, the Buzzcocks, and that summer was just it, you know, everything came into place. I took drugs, drank, slept with a woman, met Pip.

So I went back for my fifth year and walked in and everybody's got new shoes and was asking 'What did you do over the summer holidays?' I walked in with short hair and I'd slept with a woman and it was fucking incredible. You know I could have landed from outer space. I just didn't work in the fifth year. And one day I said to my mother, 'I'm not going back.' So they sent an Educational Welfare Officer, Bridie Gaskin, who decided that my problem was that I didn't fit in and she was saying, 'You've got to get your O levels, we've got to get you in somewhere.' I was wearing bits of men's suits from Oxfam and she thought that I had sexual problems, although I didn't tell anybody that I'd slept with this woman.

It was very strange how it came about. One minute I was sitting home being interviewed by Bridie Gaskin and then the next I was bundled off to this horrible flat sixties-built unit in Macclesfield, in the middle of a field opposite the Parkside, the main mental hospital. I'd done all these things, like taking drugs and that, but I wasn't prepared for the kind of kids that were in there. They had been in care since they were so young and were the kind of kids that would threaten to kill you in your sleep. I remember things like plastic sheets on your beds and I'd never wet my bed. I felt perfectly normal; I felt quite happy now I knew that I was gay and I was ready to go out in the world. But I was too young to do it. I tried to explain punk rock to the psychiatrists. They asked me what I felt about my father.

My memories of it are having to get up early, the rumpus room which was a padded room and, you know, 'Oh God Help Me' written on the walls 260 times. While I was there two of the kids topped themselves. Sexually, I didn't do anything there. I didn't join in with the girls because I was scared of showing that I was

gay. I remember the gym mats were glistening with spunk. I'd
never felt that kind of crude need in me so I just switched off. I
just started to think, 'I can look after myself, I can fool these
psychiatrists.' And you know it made me like an outsider too.
When they first decided to put me in this unit, I had to go back
to school and they had a box with 'Naylor' chalked on it; don't
know why on earth they assumed I would like my history book
etc. The Headmistress asked to see me and she was incredibly
spiteful. I went back there in black winklepickers and men's suit
trousers. It was like a western bar scene [laughs] and I went into
the classroom and said, 'Yeh, they are sending me away to a
mental hospital.' And I'd told all these girls at the beginning of
the fifth year that I'd taken drugs and rumours were around that
I was a drug-crazed maniac. I don't know, I'd like to think so.

In June my aunt Barbara died. I'd just come out of the unit;
while I'd been there nobody had contacted her and my mother got
a phone call from Barbara's school, saying she hadn't been in. My
mother went to her home and she found her sitting in a chair. My
aunty Barbara had breast cancer for two years and had not told
anybody, and she had started to hallucinate and her young son
had been looking after her. My mother brought her to Manchester
and she stayed at our house one night. I slept on the sofa
downstairs and I heard her get up in the middle of the night; she
was moaning and dragging herself around and I lay on the sofa
terrified that she'd come in. Within a week she was dead. I saw
her walk out when she went to hospital with my mother and she
was bent over and her skin was all dead and they found that she
had cancer through her body.

I'd been a bit of an arrogant little shitbag I think and it really
rocked me. My mother actually needed support; she showed
emotion and that brought us closer. They farmed out her son to
my aunty Jean, poor bastard and I haven't seen him since that
day. [Pause] Very soon afterwards – I'm sixteen now, it's the
summertime – I went to this gay club called the Picador a lot,
with butches at the bar, femmes waiting to be picked up; just
incredible. Punk hadn't permeated the gay scene yet. And then at
the end of the summer I left home, got a flat with Pip and this
girl I'd met through an advert in *Sounds*, Cath, who became my
first lover. We formed a band together. I played keyboards; I
mean I have no musical ability but it was punk rock wasn't it? I

loved it. We lived in a council flat in a very rough area in Manchester and me and Cath got eleven quid between us a week, but her father ran a market stall and we would buy job lots of egg noodles which we lived on. Cath was my first proper lover and the affair lasted for about eight months. It was never a passionate affair. It was just being young and finding out. I continued living with Cath for five years afterwards.

During that time in Manchester we were getting on with living, playing in a punk rock band, called The Gay Animals [laughs]. We supported quite a lot of big bands and we started to run a fanzine which covered sexual politics and everything, called *City Fun*, which was an excellent magazine. Me and Cath wrote for it and produced it every month for five years. I wrote a lot about sexual politics, although I was pretty anti-gay and really hated 'right on' things. Me and Cath were stupid really and we even had a picnic on the grave of one of the Moors murders victims. I think it was just a punk thing, being shocking and nasty. We were well known in Manchester because we went around everywhere together and we both wore suits, shirts, ties, but in a hip way not in a bus conductress way. We were pretty full of ourselves. I managed a band, I had a few affairs and sexually each one was a little bit better. I was growing up. I was very into drugs. I used to go to gay places – the Picador – with Pip and people would assume we were butch, but we wore suits because we were like cool punk rockers. They didn't understand. And there were a lot of transvestites and they were like nasty misogynists and they all looked very old fashioned like Dusty. There are loads of tvs in Manchester. I don't know what is it [laughs]. Manchester is the home of Fou Fou LeMarr's famous drag club. There was a club called the New Conti which was even shittier than the Picador. It was just full of like off-duty soldiers and there was a horrible tacky juke box on a stage. It's a great nightclubbing city, but it was all stopped when James Anderton Mad Methodist got in.

Q: *Why did you move to London?*

My sister moved down to the Royal College of Art to do an MA and I'd started to get very close to her, and there is a large gay scene in London and I was beginning to feel a bit isolated living with Cath I think. I wanted gay friends. Two things happened which I think made me move. One was I'd decided to become heterosexual and had a long affair with this bloke Richard. He had moved down to London too. I decided to become heterosexual because I was pissed off with women and the gay scene and I really like Richard a lot. My affair with Richard just petered out. What I hated about it was being seen as conventional; it was the first time that I'd ever been acknowledged as a couple. It never happened with women. After that I realized that I wanted to have another affair with a woman. Also that previous summer – I moved down in January – I took loads of acid. After that I thought, 'I've got to move.' So me and Cath moved down into a squat in Rotherhithe. And I really liked it, to be in London and to go to The Bell.

I used to go to this night club, the Mary Magdalene club on Great Portland Street, and pretty soon I actually got picked up by a student from the Royal College of Art. She lived in Wapping, I lived in Rotherhithe. On the tube back from the club, she didn't get out at Wapping and she said, 'Can I come home with you?' and I had an affair with her. It was my first really serious affair with a woman. I fell in love. Well, I thought I had at the time. She'd never slept with a woman before and that put a lot of onus onto me. I moved out of Rotherhithe, did a lot of moving round and I formed my own record promo company, going to papers and Radio One, trying to get records played and reviews, bands interviewed. I got very into the music biz. I was still going out with Frankie, the art student, and I was a bit of a sod to her, I think. She's a very emotional, delicate person. I was just destructive, you know, and my destruction spilled onto her. She was very adoring of me and that made me want to abuse it I think, and I was just into this cycle: work, drink, drugs, work. I'd stopped writing, which is also a bad sign. I was really working very hard.

And then Mandy walked into my office to ask me some advice about a band she knew and I immediately fell in love with her. I pretty soon moved in with her. And we embarked on a course of mutual self-destruction. It seems a bit silly to say that two people meet each other and there's something they bring out in each other, but it was like that. It was really destructive, and it was good fun; it was physical all the time. And I thought, 'This is what I want. This intensity is what I've been looking for all the time.'

We got in a car one day and we drove up north, drove through the night, and she was talking to voices of God. I was sitting in the seat next to her and it never occurred to me to stop it because I was involved with it. She was driving on the wrong side of the road at about seventy miles per hour through the night; we stopped in the Midlands, in Nuneaton where I was born, slept in a motel and she was waking up at five o'clock every morning, mumbling. In Settle, in Yorkshire, she was driving so fast I thought I was going to die. I accepted it. We hit a wall, almost wrote the car off. We limped two miles an hour to Kendal and booked into a hotel, woke the night porter. She was really very, very ill. We stayed in the Lakes for about a week and in the end we got the AA to relay us back to London. We just stayed in guest houses and hotels and got chucked out of hotels and the police would come.

I was with somebody who was schizophrenic. We got back to London and for about a week we lived at the flat. I went out one day and earlier in the morning Mandy had gone to visit a friend of her mother's, who had seen her and had put her on a plane to her mother because she was so ill. There was a note for me, 'God I really love you, I don't want to go.' I had a week on my own in the flat and I started to realize what I was involved in. She came back and her parents followed her a couple of days later and they were saying, 'You have to look after her', and I was saying, 'Yes, yes I'll do that' and I was left alone with her again. During the next month her behaviour just got worse and worse. It got so much that one morning I woke up and said, 'I'm going to Manchester.' I knew it was the last time I'd see her; she waved me off at the train. My mother wondered why I'd gone up there. I explained a little but I wasn't out to my mother. One day I got a phone call from one of her friends saying Mandy's been sectioned. And I got a message via a friend of mine to meet her and I just couldn't handle it. It was very hard and we said, 'Oh we won't see each other again.'

I was homeless then, had nothing, and I was emotionally in a really bad state but I didn't realize it. One day I woke up back in the flat. I still had my key. I didn't know how I'd got there. I got to a nearby friend and they literally put me in a bath, put me in a bed and I slept for a day in somebody's house. I was really fucked up. Friends of mine were going away and they lent me their flat for two weeks and I just literally sweated it out, wrote for the first time, wrote it out. It was just like this big destruction trip that I went on and I stayed on until I began to understand how I felt.

So eventually I just got over it. Since then I thought, I'm going to be celibate and write and get myself together, and then totally out of the blue I met Nicky. I didn't know it, but it was exactly the kind of thing that would begin to heal me I think. Suddenly the world was so brilliant, this is starting January and I was writing to my mum and in the middle of the letter I just say, 'Oh sod it, I'm happy because I'm in love. I don't think it needs to be said, but I'm a lesbian.' The letter back was very calm. She just said, 'I was overcome by your honesty.'

Last year she had cancer and she recovered from it and started climbing mountains immediately after her hysterectomy. Eighty-five was an incredible year, all those very heavy emotional things happened. I just couldn't imagine her dying. And she's getting married this year.

When I came out to my mother, I felt optimistic about my future for the first time, but being more honest with her has made our relationship more painful. I've tried to go over my childhood and adolescence with her but we haven't resolved anything; it's not as easy as 'getting to know your mother as a person'.

It's all much rawer than that.

POSTSCRIPT

This isn't the whole story: this isn't my statement. That was then, this is now, and as a lesbian, here I am.

Liz Naylor, 18 March, 1988

SUE KING

INTERVIEWED ON 5 DECEMBER 1985 BY
MARGOT FARNHAM

I was born in Kent on 9 June 1964. I've two sets of parents. My natural mother is English/half-Irish and my father is British Guyanan. There were several episodes of violence in my home, so I spent the first four years of my life in and out of a children's home. At the age of four my present parents fostered me but it didn't work out so I was then put back into the children's home and placed in various foster homes. Eventually I calmed down as an individual and the children's home placed me back with the first set of foster parents who are both white.

At eighteen I decided that I definitely wanted to know who my natural parents were. Finding out was a trauma in itself, because I had to convince the social worker that I was emotionally stable in order to find out. I had a legal guardian given to me when I was fostered and she decided to give me information regardless of what it would do to me, because I was so determined.

I don't know how to describe my natural mother. I found out that I have eight brothers and sisters. The group itself is just so varied. We've got one little Fascist who was the first born, totally white, blond hair blue eyes. He cannot stand what he classes as the 'niggers and the pakis'. And there is a real mix of nationalities. We've actually met on two or three occasions now and it's really wonderful to suddenly have what I never had when I was younger, which was brothers and sisters. I have a twin who I was separated from. I also have a brother, a gay man who I consider to be my brother because he spent a foster period with my foster parents and we got very close. Apart from my twin and

Colin, my foster brother, I didn't discover this family until I was eighteen.

When I was growing up the Social Services were not interested in placing Black children with Black families. There were various excuses like, there aren't any Black families coming forward, but I have memories of loads of Black couples coming to the children's home. We used to have a Saturday afternoon when we played with toys in a big room. This was our one afternoon of fun. We were like zoo animals and people would look around and talk to us. The whole time that we were there, you'd see Black couples. They were quite noticeable because the children's home was just outside Kent, not an area densely populated with Black people. I noticed the Black couples but I never used to notice them coming in on the Saturday, when they would come and talk to us. I actually asked when I was seven why I couldn't have a placement with a Black family, and it was seen very much as, I want to be placed with trouble-making little kids like me.

I had one very special friend in the children's home, Bernard. He was of mixed race as well. He was a very strong child and when I was very buzzy he used to be very practical, and we had a really good time together. He was an amazing kid and we kept in contact for quite a while as well. He was somebody who hadn't had violence but had had a lot of sorrow. His parents had died and he was therefore without anybody as he saw it. I remember him most because we tried to kill ourselves together. We were six. Every day we had to kneel at our beds and pray to God for forgiveness and we were told that we were evil sinners. We were terrified of ourselves. We thought we were so evil that no one would ever want to adopt us. We were just going to be stuck there for eternity. We ran away together a couple of times as well. I believe we got about 300 yards up the road with two sets of raspberry jam sandwiches [laughs]. But then we got quite tired so we thought we'd better walk back.

He was one of those pathetic kids who people always pick on and he had this tiny little afro. And I used to get bullied, so we thought if we were going to get bullied we'd get bullied together. I was a tiny kid. We found some common ground; we could work together. By getting together, there were two of us then. It wasn't just one pathetic little kid. We actually looked like some kind of competition, so people used to leave us alone.

I was adopted when I was twelve. After fostering me for quite some time, the parents that I was with decided they wanted to adopt me. They first took me when I was ten and I didn't want to play. We got up to the court and this man smoking a big cigar sat opposite and said, 'Well, little girl, how do you feel about changing your name, fitting into the family and never, ever going back?' I just sat there and said, 'No, I don't want to change my name' and so they couldn't adopt me. At that time I was latching onto my surname and I would not let go of it. I was frightened to lose any part of my Black background. It took them eighteen months to talk me round to being adopted.

The area I had moved into was Woking in Surrey and at that time it was totally white. There weren't any other Black kids at my Primary school at all. I had a lot of fears about going to my secondary school. I went with the attitude of, 'I'm going to be killed', because it was a rough school and here I was, this little kid still. I was so scared of being beaten up, that I ate myself silly and got myself into an awful physical state, but at least I started school being big and nobody picked on me. And then I got involved in sport and I just got very, very fit and I was captain of most of the school teams.

It wasn't until my Senior School that there was the 'Asian Invasion', that's what it was called at the time. It was just the start of when unemployment became a big issue, 1976, and a redevelopment plan was announced. A lot of smaller firms in Woking were shutting down, and suddenly bigger firms were deciding that they wanted their office space out of London. British American Tobacco was the first one and everybody was waiting for the next and the next. Because of the run-down state of the homes in two particular roads, everybody had just assumed that they were going to purchase the property there and turn it all into businesses and factories. What actually happened was, there was an influx of Asians into the area, into these two streets, to work in the factories just outside Woking, and they moved them into the most controversial area in the town, the area that everybody was looking to for these new businesses to start springing up. Before that, I was the only Black kid for miles. Then I started seeing racism in that place for the first time.

All of a sudden it was, 'Oh, those bloody Pakis, but you're all right.' I was very frightened. My first reaction was, 'Oh, that's all right; I'm not like "them"'', and then I thought, 'What the hell are you saying? They are like you. They're the minority, like you're the minority.' And I started to assess my politics. I felt very angry that my best-friends were beating up the Asians and I had to have a real clean sweep and start again and I dragged myself very much into the Asian community. When the Asians started coming to our school, I started building up very close friendships. We used to have a hockey team of virtually all Asian girls.

Q: *What were your permanent family like?*

I have a great amount of respect for what they did for me when I was younger. My father pushed me very much in the direction of CND and the Peace Movement. He was a pacifist during the war. I respect him for that. My dad's very loud. He's a clever man. It's just a shame that he doesn't have an ounce of common sense. He used to be a translator of veterinary documents. My mother was a librarian when she was much younger but spent the rest of her time living for him and living for me. They had fostered several children. I was the only child that they actually adopted.

As far as I can remember, I was always attracted to girls. We used to have a whole gang of us in the same street and we found it very interesting to be with each other physically as well as emotionally. Nobody put a label on it. There were about six of us who were involved with each other in various different ways. That's as far back as I can remember.

The biggest crush was when I was eleven. I was absolutely obsessed with this fifteen-year-old girl. She was a hockey goalie [laughs] at another school, and I just had to be near her. I had to join the same club that she belonged to. That was my first lesbian relationship. Looking back, it was rather amusing. At the time it was just really exciting. I suppose I felt I'd never had a big secret before. I knew I had to keep it quiet. Nobody told me I had to: I knew, and it was that feeling of doing something that I knew I shouldn't be doing, a rush of knowing that I mustn't get caught. But I was going to do it because I wanted to, and we loved being with each other and just being close to each other and taking care of each other, and also the excitement around the edge of it, of getting caught and what would happen if we did. The relationship developed slowly. I just started going over on my motorbike, illegally.

Q: *When you were eleven?*

I had a thing about bikes and I used to ride over and we went to a pub. And all of a sudden there was a whole new world to me opening out. I used to drink two pints and then we used to go up to the local park on the roundabout. We used to spin it right round and then stand in the middle of it and fall off because we were so dizzy. And we used to run across the common. We camped out a couple of nights and didn't tell anyone where we were going. We got into quite a bit of trouble: you can imagine.

I'd heard the word 'lesbian' at the hockey club, because people said about two of the workers: 'Oh, they're lesbians.' And I was totally fascinated and was looking to see if there was anything the same with me. I think I was looking for a physical sign. I felt comfortable around them and Sandy felt comfortable around them, and that was good. I thought I was a lesbian and I was frightened that I was. I knew what I was doing was classed as lesbian but I didn't want to acknowledge that word. It felt dirty. I was taught it was dirty. My father took me to the hockey practice and back and I used to hear him saying 'Bloody lesbians' and my mum would say, 'Oh, don't be silly! It can't possibly be.'

I think I chose totally the wrong time when I came out to my father. I was at Greenham and he'd come to take me home so I could have a bath. And he said something really obnoxious like, 'When are you going to get married and settle down and start being responsible?' And I just said, 'You know damn well I'm a lesbian.' At the time, we were in the middle lane of the motorway and it was a really inappropriate time because his reaction was to slam his foot down on the brake in the middle of the motorway and sit there and fume. That was the first time that I'd ever been positive with him. I'd always hidden, pretended, not said anything. He'd known for some time because I actually made a point of declaring it to my mother.

In Woking there's just no space to actually grow the way you want to. You're very pushed into one little box and if you don't fit, they're going to bang you in. It's very difficult to get out to Camberley or Guildford where there are gay groups. That's a shame because there must be loads of places like Woking where people are just choosing to conform. I tried it for a long time.

What that meant for me was that when my parents wanted to see boys at the front door, that's exactly what I gave them. But I actually selected the most obnoxious, hideous characters just to get on my parents' nerves. I started doing that at thirteen. While I was with these boys I could carry on seeing women and girls from school, but if I wasn't seeing boys I'd get the questions asked.

There were three blokes who I felt a lot for. One of them was involved in a motorbike accident and was killed. One of them, I didn't want to sleep with him. The other one I was deeply involved with and I was having lesbian relationships at the same time and feeling very confused. The only thing that helped me was when he wanted me to get married to him, I could actually say, 'No, I can't give you that because I want relationships with women.'

Q: *Can you tell me something about your political beliefs?*

My politics to do with being Black, while I was with my white middle-class family, was non-existent. Yes, I had an involvement with the Asian community: that was the first time that my politics started coming out around my colour. And then much later, when I left home, I'd suddenly found myself in London with nowhere to stay, feeling really frightened, and I got a lot of help from the Black community and a feeling that I could actually regain that bond I'd never had.

My politics are very much based on an anarchist theory. I believe that everyone can live together on this planet. I don't like rules and regulations; I think walls and barriers are things that men have put up and they're for men to take down, but if they won't, I sure as hell will.

When I was at school, I became involved in CND. My father started explaining to me the theory behind the nuclear bomb. I then got more information about the peace movement, about what people were doing to this planet, so I became fascinated with the earth. CND was trying to save the planet from being blown up: then I started looking at how we were destroying the planet and then I thought about the way men treated women. The fact that girls had less fun than boys was certainly a big thing for me when I was younger, and I started to look at that more. And I started to resent Colin, my foster brother, because he was allowed a football and a train set and I wanted a train set. I had a Tiny Tears. Our interest in each other's toys used to be really good because we were able to share. He had Lego and Meccano and I gave him a Cindy doll and horse. Colin used to love to dress dolls up and put make-up on them beautifully with pins and never scratch them. I think watching that must have been disturbing for my parents, because we just didn't seem to be conforming at all and I think, as we grew up, we became more aware of our sexuality.

When I was at school, I was actually quite a nuisance, but I didn't see it as politics, I just saw it as being fair. We'd had trouble with one particular teacher at school and there were two walkouts and one sit-in and I was basically picked out as the ringleader. The teacher had disciplined a girl – one of those girls who would never say anything out of turn – and he dragged her across the desk, lifted up her skirt and started slapping her. For anybody to be hitting anybody at this stage was out of order, but for a man to discipline a girl! Everybody just demanded that he be dealt with. The girl's parents immediately complained. She was your model student and I think that was the only reason we got away with what we did. The teacher was dismissed. That was when we suddenly realized that pupils had a say; it wasn't given to you, you had to take it.

I left school at fifteen, because I'd got O levels and it was ridiculous for me to take any more. I applied for a trainee sales consultant job, even though they wanted someone between eighteen and twenty-one. I think they were so shocked at my application that they interviewed me, and I was totally confident that I wasn't going to get the job so I said I could do it, and they took me on and decided to send me to college to do a BEC National Diploma in Business Studies, alongside training me for a sales job. Immediately I got the job I left home and there was a big scene about that. Being with my parents wasn't the right place for me. They weren't prepared to listen to me and I think a lot of that was about them realizing what sexuality I had chosen for myself. I was still seeing girls. So I left home and moved to London, although I worked in Walton-on-Thames.

The job went very well; I was very good at conning people, but

I wasn't happy with it. For your junior consultancy you had to write a programme to sell the 'service concept' and they considered mine to be something sellable, so I got my junior consultancy.

This was at a time when I'd been questioning my own politics and I was fed up with going along to these meetings of directors, looking through their personnel records and deciding that this woman and that woman had to go because they were women. That's what a lot of it came down to in electronics firms or even on the shop floor: 'That woman trying to sell that man a hi-fi isn't going to work.' And no one was prepared to re-think his attitude. It stopped being a game and started to be something quite serious. The job meant I could move away from home and that was what I wanted. I think I became more aware of what my work meant for women. And that's when I decided to go to Greenham. I had heard about Greenham from my father. That was around the time that cruise missiles were going to be arriving and I went down for two days in November '83.

There were just so many women, I thought, how wonderful to live there, and I think it really shocked me: the police shocked me, the base shocked me, the power it held, to make women react like that. Fear, I think that was the big thing. I'd had a lot of coaching by my dad and I was horrified that people in this country were allowing us to become a pawn in a game that's nothing to do with us. The feeling that came out of that base was so painful. (It's going to sound really dramatic.) It was like the earth screaming. There was beautiful forest land there, and to have lopped the trees down like that . . .

I went again at the beginning of February. I was talking to my boss and I just said, 'I'm leaving; I'm going to Greenham.' And she was so good about it. She gave me three weeks' holiday pay on top of two months I'd just had off, so it came to quite a nice little bundle. I spent a lot of it on equipment so I could go regularly to camp, and I went down for a weekend and never came back, except to sign on every two weeks.

Before I went to camp I told my mum that I was going and she was furious. Although her politics are in line with the idea, so long as it's not me it's OK. She couldn't understand how her daughter was going to go from a junior consultant to a Greenham woman. I also told her that I was committed to having a relationship with the woman I wanted to live with and she was really shocked. At first, she said 'There's no way; I can't talk to you. I don't want to see you', and I accepted that. There was nothing else I could do about it. Two weeks later, a package arrived in the post from my mum and there was just one card with it – 'I love you' – and it was a pair of Doc Marten's, and I was just so pleased. I only had money for sleeping bags and warm clothing. It had never occurred to me to get boots; I had some scruffy old plimsolls. Of course, my mum had been down to camp, taking up hot meals and had seen loads of women wearing Doc Marten boots. I'd never had a pair of boots in my life, other than motor bike boots. I melted the bottoms of them at camp but I've kept onto them and I always will, I think, because they are special to me, my mum's concession. That was as far as she could go, to say, 'I can't cope with it', but, yet, to say, 'If you're going to do it anyway, you might as well have warm feet.' It was a lovely gesture, I thought.

I arrived quite late in the evening at the main gate, and a woman came rushing over, and I felt really welcome. The next day, I felt really pushed out. I met a lot of the other women at camp who thought, Oh, you're only visitors. And then I thought, 'No, I'm not a visitor. I'm here for a reason.' I decided to stay.

Yellow Gate was certainly a mix of women. It was very exciting but I felt very on the outside of it. I think I was quite a frightened person. I learned how to feel at Greenham. I'd just shut out feelings, emotion, pain, tears. I learned that it was all right to cry and someone was just going to sit and talk to you and you could have a good laugh. A lot of CND bods who trudged up in their wellie boots and their good cheer didn't feel what women were going through in the world. They were just looking at the nuclear issue, and I think the women at camp were looking at women's issues.

There was one woman who I thought the world of. I was determined to walk round this nine-mile fence. I'd set out and I got halfway between Yellow Gate and Green Gate and I saw a woman sitting by the fence, talking to a soldier, who was scoffing about violence and they'd obviously got into a debate, so I sat down to listen to what was going on and I was totally shocked. She was telling the soldier about why she was physically violent to her children; that there was violence in everybody but we were dealing with ours and he wasn't. And I just thought, 'Is that woman crazy?' Then I started thinking, 'No, you hide a lot from women.

So it must take much more to say that to a soldier.' She was the woman who gave me this stone, that I wear round my neck. She taught me to be more honest with myself.

I found it very difficult at first to actually commit myself to non-violence; I got pulled around and kicked by the police but I managed to keep myself together and keep singing. I was involved in a couple of incidents with the police. In the first one, a policeman started throwing around my lover, who is an epileptic, and I just grabbed hold of his arm.

The other incident happened because we were fed up with the police extinguishing our fires, so we built an enormous fire and lured the police to come and put it out. Now, meantime we'd made up a concoction of washing-up water and all the old food. The police came down, four of them with fire extinguishers, squirted the fire out and as they turned to leave we just wafted this great amount of stuff all over them. At first it was taken very much as a joke. Our mistake was to follow them and torment them with it. One of the police rugby tackled one of the women, knocked her to the ground and knocked her out. My reaction was just to turn round and say, 'Officer, don't you think you've over-reacted?' 'You're nicked', was the response I got, into the van I went. In went the semi-unconscious woman. The three of us got arrested and we came up in court the next morning. Before this I'd say 'If I get arrested I'm paying the fine; I'm not going to prison.' The shock and horror on my face when I came up in that court; the police requested we be remanded in custody. I'd already made my decision I was never going to prison and there I was remanded for eight days. I was with two women who had been to prison before; it was no big deal to them and they really helped me go through that, to go through my biggest fear which is to be locked in. In Holloway they have these little cubicles that they lock you in; I suppose it's about three foot wide and maybe four and a half deep and it's just a door and there's a tiny little hole like this with glass in it and that was all you could peer through. It's like a box. You can't get out, you can't see anyone, you can't hear anyone. You can just hear footsteps, if they're just outside. It's quite terrifying but there was one woman one side, one woman the other side and they started banging on the walls and that was quite settling, to realize there was somebody I knew, and I banged back. It was after the main eviction at Yellow Gate when I went into prison.

Q: *Can you tell me your reasons for leaving the camp?*

I was thinking about bail conditions, and I didn't want to be in prison at that time. Then came a slightly different look at life I suppose. I felt that the base was holding women's attention and stopping women from doing other things. Greenham had a lot of value because we're showing that woman aren't going to stand for it. Women are backing away from Greenham and new women are coming in and I'm delighted that those women who've put in years of energy into that fence are now saying they are going to get involved in other things but still keep those connections. I still need Greenham in my life but it's going to play a different role. I'm not making it my life anymore but I'll never forget some of the good things that happened there.

I sat around for a while. After I left the camp I became active in quite a few things in a small way, and then in February 1985 I got involved with the London Lesbian and Gay Centre. In between I got in touch with certain Black groups, and became involved with LGYM (Lesbian and Gay Youth Movement), anarchist groups, and certainly squatting.

The squats were set up after a summer camp of the Lesbian and Gay Youth Movement started. There were a lot of people at the youth camp who were fed up with where they were living and wanted to squat in London, so they got together and set up the community. I find that I agree with a lot of the politics in LGYM. I wrote a really outrageous article for the magazine that I got a lot of stick for from men. And it got at the gay community and woke them up a bit; it was saying, 'You're just as shitty as straight men and I can't see the difference.'

Q: *Do you want to say something about what you expect from your relationships with women?*

It's down to sharing experiences. There are certain things about my life and about me that I feel I can only share with one woman or two women and that closeness, that knowing somebody is important to me. Physical expression is important, but I think it's very much more emotional contact. The feelings, being able to be honest.

POSTSCRIPT

After giving my life story I realized how little I knew about myself. The memories that I have are blurred images of violence and painful events that don't seem to have any order. Rehashing my life story made me look at the things that happened and more importantly the things that I subconsciously left out.

Since giving my life story I revisited my social worker, and discovered (at twenty-three) that my mother's husband – the British Guyanan – was not my father, although his name was on my birth certificate. For my 'protection' social workers have always decided to withhold the truth from me or tell me only half-truths. I still don't know who my father is. My mother has re-married, wants to forget the past, and tells me through my social worker to get on with my life. I am still totally dependent on the authorities to tell me what really happened and they have always only given me versions of my childhood which they think I can deal with. I still feel driven by the need to know basic information about my birth.

Sue King, March 1988

EPILOGUE

From the thirties to the eighties, these stories evoke those moments where the broad daylight history of news headlines resonates in the private world of individual experience. We have brought these life stories together without analysis or obvious interpretation, although we have mentioned some of the ways that experience is mediated in oral history accounts: by our questions, the speaker's sense of purpose, the editorial process; by the absence of other accounts; by the consciousness of the present. It is important to remember the context of the Hall Carpenter Archives, the circumstances of the recordings, and our approach, which was to encourage a lesbian storytelling and a restructuring of important events and developments in order to question how we develop lesbian identity.

How can the interviews be interpreted? It is impossible to list the insights offered by the life stories. Nevertheless, each speaker suggests interpretive pathways within her own story. She states the important influences on her life: a person who is loved; a lover; a parent; a book; a teacher; a political movement, whether of women or lesbians, or Black people, or for civil rights, or peace; a political development which changes the lives of a generation.

Our work exists in a historical tradition of feminist and radical popular history writing. This book is not a history of lesbian radicalism, however, but our contribution towards a questioning of lesbian identity. Elsewhere radical historians have discussed how popular memory is shaped: by the enshrinement of certain 'truths' in museums and heritage industry displays, by cinematic and television and fictional treatments, as well as shared individual memories and the conventional written sources of history. The understanding of lesbian experience, too, is influenced by cultural,

222

medical, social and political treatments. The heritage industry is unlikely to create lesbian costume dramas for the consumption of tourists; it is our absence which creates distortion. Our histories are on the whole suppressed and unlikely to be enshrined in museums, and all lesbian and feminist archives are currently starved of cash in this country. It is possible to discern within lesbian and gay circles a 'pink-plaque', celebrity-orientated approach to the past. Fortunately the women's and lesbian movements have invested much energy (given our lack of resources) into preserving the sources through which we are able to understand our past.

While lesbian history is unlikely to be institutionalized into popular memory as, for example, the Second World War has been, its understandings are still influenced by cultural and social representations. Clearly, social representations of lesbians are important to women and often women refer to them directly and indirectly: one woman says, 'I'd heard the word "lesbian" but I thought it was some form of swear word.' Another, 'I knew homosexuals existed but I didn't know what the hell they were: spinsters who wore tweed skirts and brogues.' We are also anxious not to be seen as having negative lives or to have others' interpretations imposed upon our experience. Myrtle discusses the change in her weight following problems with her thyroid as a young woman: 'But no way will I allow anybody to say that made me become a lesbian. It's true that I was no longer attractive to men, but that was a relief in a way.' Another woman discusses her silence on sexual abuse and the fear that her sexuality will be attributed to this act of violence. Diana tells the story of when Kenric members became subjects in a test to discover whether there were physiological and psychological differences between lesbians and heterosexual women. 'It transpired that they could find no significant differences . . . What they did say, though, was that lesbians evinced far worse relationships with their parents . . . we hate our parents. Now they would probably redesign the test.' Diana talks about the fifties, the heyday for the expert: '. . . every book I ever read (and I had a stack of those blue Pelicans) told me that it was immature . . .'

Women place their experience in a clearly perceived historical context. 'I was born round about the same time as *The Well of Loneliness* was going to the printers.' The author's authorities for this book are all experts who hold a congenital model of lesbianism: Krafft-Ebing, Magnus Hirschfeld. Even though the work of these experts belongs to a previous period, their messages are taken up by Diana because *The Well of Loneliness* is an important influence on her life.

There are also popular stereotypes about lesbians whose origins are more difficult to place but which are nevertheless powerful. Zerrin articulates the concern of many Black women and lesbian mothers: 'the anthology will show that it is not just a white history and will shatter the myths about lesbians and motherhood.' It is difficult and often dangerous for women, especially mothers, to define themselves outside the family. Sharley faces this conflict when she first struggles to recognize that she is a lesbian: 'I'm married. I've got two kids. How can I?'

Throughout the stories there is an insistence that we understand the contexts for the periods of time women are dealing with.

'I think the fifties were a bloody awful decade, especially for women.'

'Independence Day came and I remember in 1947 when the Union Jack came down at school.'

'It was just the start of when unemployment became a big issue in 1976.'

'The Civil Rights Movement in America and Sharpeville had a particularly strong impact.'

'We were influenced by the hippy movement, though we couldn't drop out as we had to earn a living.'

Time is bridged. Contexts change. To emphasize the difference between the present and the wartime period, Sharley comments: 'I think we were naive sexually.' To explain important changes in herself and society during one period of her life, Megan observes: 'When I entered the convent it was Donny Osmond, when I came out it was Sid Vicious.' Liz talks about key experiences of her adolescence: punk, and her experience of a young person's psychiatric unit: 'I was fifteen and punk was about to happen.' Then we are introduced to the psychiatric practices of a previous decade: 'this horrible flat sixties-built unit in Macclesfield.'

Many speakers direct us to their parents' histories so that we are able to understand the complexities of certain episodes in their own life. Joyce felt as a child that she needed to look after her mother: 'I wonder if it wasn't just the totally different expectations of society over here. In Jamaica she had her first child when she was about thirteen.' Susan traces a connection between her mother's thirties progressive background and her own adolescent free love approach to sex. Her mother's progressive attitudes, however, are permeated with Freudianism and her mother's view colours the way Susan is able to see the single lesbian teachers at her school and later her own sexuality.

As well as referring to social representations about lesbians, many women refer to or question public ideas about the ethnic or cultural group they are a part of. Susan talks about her parents' conservatism, the side of them she finds unlikeable. 'To try and understand that, there was the Holocaust . . . I think they did have incredibly strong feelings of insecurity, of having to pass and make it in the world.' Gilli talks about her father's alcoholism: 'In colonial countries the men of the mixed race community often abuse alcohol.'

The speakers also offer interpretive symbols, signs or motifs which recur or remain as backcloths, both to illuminate or to understand their experience and to underline their life's concerns. Helen, whose life is very involved with the Labour movement, recollects her childhood: 'One of the first things I remember was the miners' lodge banner.' Megan explores a conflict in her life between her need for individual expression and her need for community. It is a conflict which centres on uniformity. 'He (my father) had a very uniformed past.' When Zerrin recalls the scare of enemy-poisoned fruit as a child during the Cyprus war, she repeats a story common to many wartime situations. In the context of Zerrin's life, however, the image of poisoned fruit resonates powerfully because she is sexually abused by her father. Her mother issues warnings about public danger, but is unable to clearly warn her about or protect her from private danger. Instead her mother has to plan courageously but carefully to make their escape.

In other places, women signpost areas for further exploration which they know of but have not themselves experienced. There are the generation of women who lived before the times observed first-hand in this anthology. Myrtle speaks of the obvious lesbians she knew who drove ambulances during the Second World War and suggests that women found certain freedoms in the First World War as well. She also talks of an older generation of suffrage campaigners, many of whom were lesbians. Women point beyond this anthology to other women's lives and achievements which have an impact on ours today.

We hope that we have revealed the many experiences of women being sustained by other lesbians and their own lesbian selves. But not everything about our past can be celebrated. Lesbians receive many negative messages that encourage an amnesiac or fractured relationship with the past. This is our contribution to a history which aims to restore memory as a process of constant re-evaluation of the past.

We want to stress our role as collectors of stories. We want to emphasize that, rather than imposing interpretations on each other's stories, we should look first at the directions offered by the speaker herself. The journeys are different. We offer this book with the hope that other more specific histories will be created.

INDEX